# Main Trends in Interdisciplinary Research

*the text of this book is printed
on 100% recycled paper*

# Main Trends in
# INTER-DISCIPLINARY RESEARCH

Jean Piaget

HARPER TORCHBOOKS
HARPER & ROW, PUBLISHERS
NEW YORK, EVANSTON, SAN FRANCISCO, LONDON

# Contents

# Introduction

The pages which follow will be continually inspired by a certain structuralism – one which we have chiefly developed since they were written (see the little *Que sais je*, 'Le Structuralisme', 4th edn 1970), and which seems to us to be common to the sciences of man and to those which are often described as 'exact and natural'. In the areas of logico-mathematics and physico-chemistry it is essentially a question of operative structures, which are, however, always interdependent with a constructivism outside which they lose their explanatory meaning. Starting at the level of biology and in all the sciences of man, structures involve a character of autoregulation in the cybernetic sense of the term, and we have become accustomed to describe this study of autoregulatory structures by the term 'genetic structuralism'. In his book *Marxism and Human Sciences*, Goldmann writes: 'We have . . . defined the positive method in human sciences, and more precisely the Marxist method, with the help of a term . . . (which we have borrowed from Jean Piaget) genetic structuralism'. We should only like to note, in making this connexion, that, if there is an effective relationship between constructivist, dialectic and structuralist methods – so long as one does not separate structures from their function and their origin – it is that the positive character that one can find in certain forms of dialectic depends on resorting to phenomena of autoregulation which are the constituents of all formative development, and that these regulations are themselves the antecedents of the autoregulating (*autoréglage*) which is characteristic of the whole operative activity of the human subject in its logico-mathematical constructions as well as in its explanatory or causal models.

When we speak of 'structures', in the most general sense of the term (mathematical, etc), our definition will nevertheless remain limiting in the sense that it will not include any static 'form' at all. We shall, indeed, give to this idea the three following characteristics: a structure implies first of all laws of totality distinct from those of its elements, which even permit complete disregard of those elements; secondly, its properties as a whole are laws of transformation as contrasted with any formal laws; thirdly, every structure implies an *autoréglage* in the double sense that its compositions do not go outside its own frontiers and that they make no appeal to anything outside such frontiers. However, this does not prevent the structure from being able to divide itself into sub-structures which inherit its characteristics but at the same time show their own individual characteristics. In its final state (as opposed to its eventual states of formation and construction) a structure constitutes therefore a 'closed' system, while at the same time it is able in its turn to integrate itself into new and wider structures, as a sub-structure. This 'closing' assures its autonomy and its intrinsic powers. When Lazarsfeld (*Main Trends*, vol. 1, p. 58) says: 'One sometimes has the impression that Piaget thinks that wherever mathematical models are used they are by definition part of the structural movement', he is mistaken about our ideas: in the field of mathematics we think that we remain faithful to the spirit of Bourbaki, whose structuralism is highly specific, and to the later researches on 'categories' of McLane, Eilenberg, etc.

One last remark. In Section 1 there will be found a defence of the idea that there is no hierarchy in the science of man, as one finds partially in the natural sciences (subordination of chemistry to physics or of biology to physico-chemistry, etc.). R. Jakobson holds an opposite view and naturally sees in his own discipline the key science which makes certain the passage of biological information (code ADN) to the human sciences which linguistics would dominate in one way or another. But he has hardly convinced us, and for two reasons. Firstly because, as Chomsky has shown, language is subordinate to intelligence or its logic and not the other way round, as contemporary positivism used to believe. However important psycholinguistics may be, especially in its psychogenetic aspects, it is thus impossible to subordinate the psychology of the cognitive functions to linguistics. Secondly, the genetic code ADN is a system of indica*ted* and not of indica*ting* (except, naturally, for the biologist as a subject of knowledge) and the information that it transmits belongs to such a system. [1] To say that the theory of information forms in this case a fundamental interdisciplinary instrument (which does not go as far as a necessary imperialism) is one thing, but it certainly does not involve attributing these powers to linguistics itself, for information and language are far from being synonymous! We shall, therefore, more than ever stand by our model of a circular, and not a linear, classification.

J. Piaget

[1] In his famous work on the fundamentals of language (*Ourkring sprogteoriens Grundlaeggelse*, Copenhagen, 1943) Hjelmslev has, in effect, shown that a language necessarily postulates the presence of two plans not in accordance one with each other (a lack of univocal correspondence and also duality of nature between indicating and indicated (*signifiant* and *signifié*); this prevents us from classifying as *languages* structures like those of algebra, or the genetic code, etc.

# Interdisciplinary Research

Interdisciplinary research can result from two sorts of inquiry, one relating to common structures or mechanisms and the other to common methods, although both sorts may of course be involved equally. As an example of the former we could quote this or that analysis of linguistic structuralism leading to the question as to whether the elementary structures discovered have any relationship with logic or with the structures of intelligence; this kind of question has been revived in the works of N. Chomsky,[1] for, contrary to the 'positivist' view that logic can be reduced to language, this author returns to the traditional subordination of grammar to 'reason'. As an example of the latter sort of inquiry or the two combined, we could quote the many applications of 'games theory', initially peculiar to econometrics. As this mathematical procedure can be applied to many psychological behaviours (problem solving, thresholds of perception, etc.) it was only natural that econometrists and psychologists should conduct joint research on economic behaviour itself. This is the case with the works of R. D. Luce (*Individual Choice Behavior*, N.Y., Wiley & Sons, 1959) and S. Siegel and L. E. Fouraker (*Bargaining and Group Decision Making*, N.Y., McGraw Hill, 1960).

In this volume, special attention will be paid to common mechanisms.

## I. POSITION OF THE PROBLEMS

### 1. *Interdisciplinary collaboration in the natural sciences*

In order to understand the situation of the social and human sciences it is essential to start by examining that of the natural sciences, for the differences separating these two situations, seen from the interdisciplinary point of view, are instructive and do not appear to be due solely to the fact that the natural sciences have a lead of a few centuries over the human sciences.

Two differences, which still obtain but may diminish in the future, oppose the natural sciences to the nomothetic sciences of the manifold forms of human behaviour. On the one hand, the former involve a hierarchical order, not of course as regards their importance, but as regards the filiation of ideas and their decreasing or increasing generality and complexity. On the other hand, by their very development they give rise to all manner of problems of reduction or non-reduction of phenomena of the 'higher' degree to those of the 'lower' degree. In view of these two circumstances, each specialist is obliged continually to look beyond the frontiers of his own discipline.

No doubt the natural sciences do not all follow a linear order and disciplines such as astronomy, with its many chapters, or geology, can only find their place on the lateral branches of the common trunk. But there is a common trunk and, going from mathematics to mechanics, then to physics and from there to chemistry, biology and physiological psychology, we can certainly discover in the main a series of decreasing generality and increasing complexity in accordance with Auguste Comte's famous criteria. Without entering into the arguments of various kinds to which such a classification can give rise, we shall deduce from it but two facts beyond dispute. The first is that one would seek in vain a similar order in the human sciences today, and so far no one has suggested such a thing. One can hardly imagine placing linguistics before economics, or vice versa, for example.[2] The second is that each of the specialists in these natural sciences actually needs a fairly good grounding in the disciplines preceding his own in that hierarchical order and often even needs the collaboration of research workers belonging to these preceding sciences, which leads to the latter taking an interest in the problems raised by the following sciences.

Thus a physicist is constantly in need of mathematics, and theoretical physics, while lending itself to experimentation, is essentially mathematical in its technique. Conversely, mathematicians are often concerned with physics and they are responsible for a 'mathematical physics' which, despite its name, is not experimental but solves by deduction some of the problems posed by physics. Nor would a chemist go far without physics: theoretical chemistry is often called 'physical chemistry'. Similarly, a biologist needs chemistry, physics, mathematics, etc. In all these fields, therefore, interdisciplinary research is becoming increasingly imperative by the nature of things, given the hierarchy of scales of phenomena, which corresponds to the hierarchical order of disciplines. Whole sciences such as contemporary biophysics or biochemistry are the inevitable products of this situation.

But although even here we have a rather different picture from that of the human sciences, another contrast is even more striking. In some of the social sciences there is certainly a tendency to reduce or, more precisely, annex, for the 'reduction' desired is generally in the direction of the science represented by the author. Sociologists have been known to reduce everything to sociology, for example. However, no economist has, to our knowledge, claimed that the facts studied by him can be reduced to linguistics (or vice versa). Now in the natural sciences, by very reason of the hierarchical filiations to which we have just referred, the problem of reduction is constantly coming up, according to the order indicated above. Consequently interdisciplinary trends receive a continual impetus.

This certainly does not mean that everyone is of the same opinion or that any problem of reduction actually leads to three possible solutions. But these very possibilities result in a closer investigation of the problems so that all three lead to interdisciplinary discussions. These solutions are: 1) reduction from the 'higher' to the 'lower'; 2) irreducibility of the phenomenon of the 'higher' level; and 3) reciprocal assimilation by partial reduction of the 'higher', but also by enrichment of the 'lower' by the 'higher'.

Many examples of these three kinds of solution are to be found. For instance, Auguste Comte is known to have considered chemistry as necessarily separate from physics because the phenomenon of 'affinity' did not seem to him to be reducible to the known mechanisms. History has shown, on the contrary, that reduction was possible, and even necessary. On questions on which the current state of knowledge remains 'open', such as the relations between life and physico-chemistry, biologists are divided between the three trends. Some are of the opinion that there can only be reduction to the physico-chemical phenomena known at present, and the new links discovered between unorganized and living bodies confirm them in this way of thinking. Others are of the opinion that the vital phenomenon remains irreducible, but in order to defend this vitalism against the former tendency they are of course obliged to study possible connexions with chemical or physical facts just as closely. Others again quote opinions such as that expressed by the physicist Ch. E. Guye in his *Frontières entre la biologie et la physico-chimie*. According to this profound author, reductions on the physical terrain itself consist almost always in the subordination of the simple to the complex, as well as the converse, in a finally reciprocal co-ordination, so that if a physico-chemical explanation of life can be expected, our present physico-chemistry will gain new properties thereby, thus becoming more 'general' instead of being applied exclusively to more and more special fields.

Analysis of such thought-processes in the development of explanations – those which have already proved acceptable and also those which are anticipated – is very instructive for our purposes. On the one hand, it shows the reasons for interdisciplinary collaboration in branches where it has become current practice and where its usefulness needs no further proof. But on the other hand, it overcomes at the outset any prejudices we might have and it dispels the belief that any connexion going beyond the frontiers of our own discipline is likely to lead to exaggerated reductions and to a weakening of the specific character of the phenomena under study. In particular, when we realize that 'it is the scale which gives rise to the phenomenon' – a fact fully brought home by the same physicist cited above – relationships established between processes on different scales both explain very well and respect the specific aspects. The first half of this century witnessed a series of partly sterile arguments between the two human sciences best fitted to co-ordinate their findings – psychology and sociology. We shall see, in section 16 and elsewhere, how, in this particular matter, the method of establishing mutual relationships has made it possible to dismiss a number of false problems and, on certain points, achieve an as yet very small measure of collaboration.

As for the hierarchies which might be established between the human sciences, this of course remains an open question so long as the central problem of sociology, that of society considered as a whole and the relations between the sub-systems and the whole system, is still not solved. Meanwhile, each discipline employs parameters which are strategic variables for other disciplines, and this opens up a vast field of research for interdisciplinary collaboration; but as there is no linear breakdown of the system into sub-systems, collaboration is only too often reduced to mere juxtaposition. On the other hand, it is very likely that new light will be thrown on the problem of the hierarchy of scales of phenomena and the related studies by the future progress of two essentially synthetic disciplines and their repercussions on the question of infrastructures and superstructures. These are ethnology, the multidimensional character of which is manifest, and history, regarded not as the mere reconstitution of events, but as interdisciplinary research dealing with the diachronic aspects of each of the fields studied by the various human sciences. As these various aspects are of course interdependent, it can be hoped that, when history eventually achieves nomothetic status, its lessons, combined with those of ethnology and sociology in general, will bring us nearer to solutions of the central problem of the relations between the sub-systems. The future of interdisciplinary research in the human sciences (with or without hierarchy) depends not only on these solutions, but on many internal questions peculiar to the various disciplines (macro- and micro-economics, etc.).

## 2. *Convergence of problems within the human sciences and their relative affinity with those of the life sciences*

A number of circumstances explains why interdisciplinary research in the social and human sciences, although generally recognized as having a great future, is not taken nearly so far as in the natural sciences. We have just had the two main and basic reasons. But to these must be added at least two kinds of contingent circumstances which have, even if contingent, played an undisputed historic rôle. One is the tragic splitting up of courses among university faculties which are more and more cut off from each other, or even among sections within these faculties, but watertight nonetheless. Whereas in a science faculty the training of any specialist requires a more or less extensive culture, a psychologist may know nothing about linguistics, economics, or even sociology. If an economist is trained in a law school, he may be completely ignorant of linguistics, psychology, etc. Whereas some universities, such as that of Amsterdam, for instance, in an effort to combat this partitioning, have placed philosophy in an inter-faculty institute so as to re-establish contact between it and the natural and social sciences, nothing similar yet exists, to our knowledge, to co-ordinate the disciplines with which we shall be dealing here.

The second factor of a general nature which has weighed on the human sciences in the past is the idea that going over the bounds of one's own discipline implies a synthesis and that the discipline specializing in synthesis, if any can be said to do so (and the very fact of expressing oneself in this way shows the weakness of such an assumption), is no other than philosophy itself. Now philosophy certainly includes a position of synthesis, which relates, however, to the co-ordination of all human values, and not to the co-ordination of knowledge alone. Consequently if disciplines such as scientific psychology or sociology have after much difficulty achieved their independence by opposing experimental or statistical test methods to methods of abstract reasoning, it is not in order to return to these methods when interdisciplinary links imposed by the facts and not by the desire for systematization are involved.

Nevertheless, if we want to have an idea of the future of interdisciplinary research between sciences all of which have their tried methods of approach and testing, but are not yet accustomed by tradition to what is now current practice in the natural sciences, the best course is perhaps to begin by comparing their problems.

Here we are immediately struck by three fundamental facts: firstly, the convergence of certain general problems, which are to be found in all the sectors of our huge field; secondly, the fact that these general problems have little connexion with those of the inorganic world, but do link up fairly directly with certain central questions of the life sciences; thirdly, that in order to solve these problems, we must have recourse to certain cardinal ideas which actually rest on common mechanisms. If all this is true, we see immediately to what extent the study of these common mechanisms demands, and will increasingly demand, a concerted interdisciplinary effort which should be encouraged in every way, among the human sciences of course, but sometimes also in relation to biology.

First of all, confining ourselves to the most general problems, there is little doubt that the three questions most central and most specific of the biological sciences (for they have little significance on the physico-chemical level) are: 1) that of the development, or evolution in the sense of gradual production, of organized forms with qualitative transformations at different stages; 2) that of organization in its balanced or synchronic forms; and 3) that of the exchanges between the organism and its environment (physical environment and other organisms). In other words, the three cardinal ideas expressing the principal facts to be explained are: 1) that of the *production of new structures*; 2) that of *equilibrium*, but in the sense of regulation and self-regulation (and not merely the balance of forces); and 3) that of *exchange*, in the sense of material exchange, but equally (for this is also the language of contemporary biologists)[3] the exchange of information.

It is worth noting that the study of these central problems is conducted more and more in the light of three instrumental methods inspired more or less directly by the human sciences, or in any case by human activities. Although there is no common semantic correspondence between these problems and methods (each method helps to solve each problem), those methods are games or decision theories (Waddington refers in this connexion to the 'strategy of genes'), information theory in general, and cybernetics to the extent that it concerns communication, guidance or control.

This being the case, it is evident that these three problems of transformation (particularly diachronic transformations), balancing and exchanges are also the three principal questions encountered in all the human sciences. Not only are they encountered in very specific forms in each of those sciences, but also the relations between the diachronic and the synchronic dimension differ very significantly according to the type of phenomenon studied: structural linguistics has thus revealed, since F. de Saussure, that the meaning of words at a given moment in history depends much more on the total system of the language seen from the standpoint of its synchronic balance than on its etymology or its history. In the psychological development of an individual, on the contrary, the final balance of the structures of the mind, for instance, depends much more on the balancing process which characterizes the whole of its previous development. Economic history, for its part, when it studies the price of wool on the London market in the thirteenth century or that of pepper in Lisbon in the sixteenth, does not see an explanation of the prices of these commodities on the same markets today, but attempts to throw light on these examples from history by recourse to the synchronic dimension, which predominates in questions of values.[4] On the other hand, problems of economic structure, as opposed to economic situations, depend upon another kind of relationship between the diachronic and the synchronic. Exchange problems, too, whether they be exchanges with the environment in physical or mental production or exchanges between individuals, are common to all the human sciences. And they combine in very different ways with the various processes – diachronic or evolutionary and synchronic or self-controlling.

This convergence of problems does not of course mean that the human sciences can be reduced to the life sciences. The former remain specific because of the existence of cultures transmitted socially and involving an inextricable complex of factors. But if this specificity in itself raises a question, this is no reason for not starting with common problems, all the more since, as we shall see, their solutions are neither uniform, which would render their terms simply trivial, nor uniformly different from one discipline to another, which would deprive their comparison of interest, but are to be differentiated from one type of structure or phenomenon to another, which means on the contrary that interdisciplinary research is essential.

## 3. *From problems to general processes: structures, functions and meanings*

The first question to be discussed in connexion with the principal problems which have just been mentioned is that of the criterion for this choice and consequently of its exhaustive or arbitrary nature. We have a striking example to guide us in this connexion: that of the determination of elementary structures (so-called 'mother-structures') by the Bourbaki school in mathematics. In order to determine these fundamental structures, from which all the others are supposed to derive by combination or differentiation, these well-known authors, although working in a purely deductive science the exactitude of which is universally recognized, state that the only method they could follow was inductive and not *a priori*. It was by simple procedures of systematic comparison (creation of isomorphisms) and regressive analysis that they arrived at three structures which could not be reduced to one another, it remaining an open question whether or not further structures should one day be added. In this particular case one could not *a fortiori* proceed differently. This simply means that the other central ideas which might be added to those of production of structures, balancing and exchange, seem in the present state of affairs to be reducible to them. For instance, the idea of 'direction', which is so important (in biology, in developmental psychology, etc.) appears to be the result of a compromise between the production of structures and their gradual balancing, when the situations are sufficiently analysed.[5]

This being the case, let us see what our three ideas stand for. First of all, when we compare the use of the term 'structure' in the various natural and human sciences[6] we find the following characteristics. Structure is, in the first place, a system of transformations having its laws, as a system, these therefore being distinct from the properties of the elements. In the second place these transformations have a self-regulating device in the sense that no new element engendered by their operation breaks the boundaries of the system (the addition of two numbers still gives a number, etc.) and that the transformations of the system do not involve elements outside it. In the third place, the system may have sub-systems by differentiation from the total system (for example, by a limitation of the transformations making it possible to leave this or that character constant, etc.) and there may be some transformations from one sub-system to another.

However, from the standpoint of the various disciplines, two kinds of structure must immediately be distinguished. The first are completed, because the way in which they are produced comes under the head of inventive deduction or axiomatic decision (logico-mathematical structures) or physical causality (for example, 'group' structures in mechanics, etc.), or because these structures constitute the form of final or momentarily stable equilibrium of a previous mental development (structures of the mind) or social development (juridical structures, etc.). The second, on the contrary, are in the process of constitution or reconstitution; the ways in which these structures are produced come under the head of vital processes (biological structures) or a spontaneous or 'natural' human genesis (as opposed to formalizations): mental or social structures in the formative stage, etc.

The preceding definition can be applied forthwith to the former of these two categories, for we are concerned here with completed structures, hence structures closed in on themselves. In this case the whole 'production' of the structure becomes one with its internal transformations, without there being any necessity for distinguishing formation and transformation, since a completed structure is at the same time structured and indefinitely 'structuring'. In the second place, the self-regulating system of the structure accounts for its 'balance', its stability being due to the laws governing that structure, or to a set of 'norms'. There is thus no need to distinguish structures and functions (in the biological and not the mathematical sense of the term), for the functioning of the structure is reduced to its internal transformations. In the third place, there are no 'exchanges', except those of an internal nature, which take the form of possible (and mutual) transitions between one sub-structure and another.

On the contrary, in the case of structures in the formative stage or in the process of continual reconstitution (as with metabolism in biology) or of momentary reconstitution, the three characteristics – production, balance and exchanges – appear in appreciably different aspects, although the forms just described may be regarded as the extremes of those with which we shall be concerned, the essential distinction between the two being that the former correspond to a stable completion and the latter to processes or developments.

In the first place, the production of the structure appears in two forms, the second being the end-result of the first: a formation and transformations. Consequently the organism, the thinking being or the social group, builders of structures, are only centres of functioning (or structuration) and not completed structures containing all possible structures by a sort of 'pre-formation'.[7] In other words, a distinction should be drawn in this formative process between the function as a 'structuring' activity and the structure as a structured result.

In the second place, in the case of structures in the formative stage, the self-regulating system can no longer be reduced to a set of rules or norms characterizing the completed structure: it consists of a system of regulation or self-regulation, with correction of errors after the event, and not the 'pre-correction' to be found in the final system (where self-regulation, moreover, marks the extreme of the self-regulation which functions during the formative stages).

Lastly, in the case of structures in the process of constitution or continual reconstitution (as with biological structures), exchange is no longer limited to internal reciprocities, as is the case between the sub-structures of a completed structure, but involves a considerable proportion of exchange with the outside, to enable these structures to obtain the supplies necessary for their functioning. This is so with structures in the formative stage, as regards the development of the intelligence, when the subject must constantly have recourse to trial and error (even in the case of specifically logico-mathematical experiments, when the information is drawn not from the objects as such but from the actions exerted upon them). This is especially so with biological structures, which are elaborated solely by constant exchanges with the environment, by means of those mechanisms of assimilation of the environment to the organism and adjustment of the latter to the former which constitute the transition from organic life to behaviour and even mental life.

A living structure, as Bertalanffy has shown, constitutes an 'open' system in the sense that it is preserved through a continual flow of exchanges with the outside world. Nevertheless, the system does have a cycle closing in on itself in that its components are maintained by interaction while being fed from outside. Such a structure can be described statically since it is preserved despite its perpetual activity, but as a rule it is dynamic since it constitutes the more or less stable form of continual transformations.

Considered from the standpoint of its activity, therefore, an 'organized' structure has a way of functioning which is the expression of the transformations characteristic of it. The word 'function' is usually applied to the rôle (sector of activity or sector of functioning) played by a sub-structure in the functioning of the total structure and, by extension, the action of the total functioning on that of the sub-structures.

Any functioning involves production, exchange and balancing, that is, it continually presupposes decisions or choices, information and regulation. The result is that, even in the biological field as such, the very ideas of structure and function carry with them the derived ideas of functional utility or value and meaning.

In the first place, any function or functioning involves choices or selections among the internal or external elements. Consequently an element can be said to be useful when it enters as a component into the cycle of the structure, and harmful if it threatens or interrupts the continuity of the cycle. But two sorts of functional utility or 'value' must be distinguished:

1. Primary utility, that is, the utility of an internal or external element (production or exchange) in relation to the structure concerned, but insofar as this element has a qualitative effect on the production or preservation of the structure as an organized form; for example, the utility of a food containing calcium for bone preservation or the utility of a group of genes in a genetic recombination likely to survive.

2. Secondary utility, related to the cost or gain stemming from the element which is useful in sense 1: cost of a transformation, of an exchange, etc., in its functioning.

Consequently this distinction refers, on the one hand, to the relational or formal aspect of the structures, hence to the structural aspect as such, and, on the other hand, to the energetic aspect of the functioning. These two aspects are of course inseparable, for there is no structure without functioning, and vice versa. But they are different, for in any production and in any exchange it is necessary to distinguish a) what must be produced or what must be acquired or exchanged, having regard to the structures to be maintained or built up; and b) what that production or exchange costs or earns having regard to the energy available.

Yet another distinction should be made as we review these general principles of biology capable of serving as a background for the analysis of the common mechanisms peculiar to the various human sciences. This distinction relates to the rôle of information, the latter being necessary for production, as it is for exchanges and control:

1. Information can be *immediate,* when a stimulus identified at once provokes a response forthwith, which means that spatio-temporal distance is abolished.

2. Information can, on the contrary, be *mediate* if there is an encoding in accordance with a fixed code and a decoding which occurs later (which means that spatio-temporal distance is not zero). The genetic information stored in germinal materials (deoxyribonucleic acid or DNA, whose code is made up of sequences, as Watson and Crick discovered in 1953) is described in this way.

Special mention should be made of the 'signals' (*indices significatifs*) which release instinctive behaviour (Lorenz, Tinbergen, Grassé and others).

It is therefore essential to take into account the idea of *communication* in addition to the structures and values of functioning, insofar as it is possible that a given element cannot be integrated as such, at least at once, in an existing structure or may have no direct or immediate functional value, but can constitute the representative or announcer of subsequent structurations or functioning. Two cases have then to be distinguished: a) the representative is not recognized as such by the organism, in other words, it does not affect behaviour, but participates in a kind of storage or reserve of information, which is used later – it is in this sense that we speak of genetic information etc.; or the transmission of information which characterizes the feedback as opposed to the main energetic process the adjustment of which is controlled by the feedback; b) this representative is used in 'behaviour' and thus becomes a signalling stimulus, etc. This brings us to the threshold of the systems of messages affecting human behaviour.

In all, we thus have before us three broad categories of ideas: *structures* or forms of organization; *functions*, sources of qualitative or energetic values; and *messages*. All three of course give rise to problems which may be diachronic – problems of evolution and construction – or synchronic – problems of balance and control, or problems of exchanges with the environment – but obviously the relations between the diachronic and the synchronic dimensions cannot be the same, according as to whether structures, functional utilities or messages are in question.

What should be done in order to enter upon the analysis of the common mechanisms considered by the various human sciences is thus to translate this general theory into terms of human behaviour. Here a preliminary remark is called for. The production, regulation or exchange which occurs in the forms we have just reviewed may be organic as much as mental or intra-physic, and we started speaking of the organic as our initial frame of reference. Although most of the human sciences deal with human behaviour without attempting to delimit in detail what is conscious and what is unconscious, the disciplines in which an explicit relationship between mind and body can continually give rise to problems, as in psychology, have moved in the direction of parallelism and isomorphism. We can interpret the 'psycho-physiological parallelism' in terms of a more general isomorphism between *causality*, the field of application of which is actually restricted to matter, and *implication* in the broad sense, which is the *sui generis* relation uniting messages peculiar to the conscious state. The few general ideas referred to in the present section should be viewed in terms of conscious implications.

## 4. *Laws, values and signs*

While all the human sciences deal with production, regulation and exchange and all use for this purpose the ideas of structure, functional utility and meaning envisaged diachronically and synchronically by turns, these ideas appear in different forms according as the researcher takes a theoretical or abstract standpoint, or again takes into account the behaviour of the subjects and even the way in which that behaviour impacts upon their minds. From the first of these two standpoints the specialist will seek the most objective language to describe structures. This he will do in varying terms but as a rule they will be capable of formalization or of mathematical expression. For instance, he will describe kinship structures in terms of algebraic systems, in the same way as Lévi-Strauss; transformational grammars in terms of monoids, in the same way as Chomsky; or micro- and macro-economic structures in terms of contingency or cybernetic diagrams, etc. However, none of all this directly affects the mind of the subject.

On the contrary, in the psychological research which we are pursuing concerning the development of the intelligence in the child and the adolescent, we also try of course to translate into abstract language the structures of intellectual operations evidenced by the behaviour of the subjects, and we use for this purpose various logico-mathematical structures coming under the head of 'groups', 'networks' and 'groupings'; but we also try to discover the form these structures take in the minds of the subjects,[8] insofar as their reasoning is expressed in words and is accompanied by various intentional justifications: what we discover is of course no longer an abstract structure but a set of intellectual *rules* or norms which take the form of impressions of 'logical necessity', etc. When a sociologist of law investigates why a legal system (formalizable or codifiable as a 'pure' normativist construction in the manner of Kelsen) is 'recognized' as valid by the subjects of laws, he is confronted with a series of bilateral or multilateral relations such as that a 'right' for some corresponds to an 'obligation' for others, etc., and what these facts imply is in turn expressed in terms of specific rules. When a logician axiomatizes a certain number of operations with the consequences which derive from them, he does not have to pay the slightest attention to the subject who performs them. But he may perfectly well concern himself with the normative aspect of the connexions he is manipulating and may even end by constructing, with Ziembinski, Weinberger, Peklov, Prior and others, a logic of 'norms'[9] (and even, with Weinberger, applying it to the legal norm).[10] Likewise, linguistic structures are translated in the consciousness of subjects by rules of grammar, even if this translation is inadequate, as indeed are many other translations (through realization) of structures in the form of rules.

The general and interdisciplinary problems that are going to arise in this connexion (see sections 5 to 9 below) now become evident at once: comparison of various types of structures, comparison of systems of rules (depending on whether these systems come close to the methods of logical composition or diverge from them in the direction of simple constraints or miscellaneous dominances), comparison of various translations or realizations of structures in the form of rules (adequate or inadequate, and why), etc.

Another major system of notions concerning the actual experiences of individuals in their mental life or in their collective relations is the system of *values* or realization of functional utility which we mentioned in section 3 above. The remarkable thing, showing once more the profound unity of reactions of all living beings in the social and human as well as the biological spheres, is that the distinction between primary utility or utility relative to the qualitative aspects of production or of the conservation of structures, and secondary utility or that relative to the energetics of functioning, recurs in the sphere of experienced values in the form of what we shall call 'values of finality' and 'values of yield'.

Values of finality include, in particular, normative values which are determined by rules: a moral value such as those which, in all human societies, distinguish actions judged to be good from those judged to be bad or indifferent, refers of necessity to a system of rules. The same applies *a fortiori* to legal values. In the sphere of individual or collective representations, judgements are valorized as true or false (bivalent values) or true, false, or plausible but not yet determinable, etc. (trivalent or polyvalent values) in terms of the accepted rules. Notions are elaborated, accepted or rejected by virtue of multiple value judgements and, while constituting structures, are constantly valorized, but once again in terms of overall normative structures. Aesthetic values do not depend on rules as imperative as these, but nevertheless refer to more or less regulated structures. On a more individual level, a subject's interest in a particular group of objects or a particular kind of work in the form of miscellaneous finalities may be remote from any normative structure and depend solely on regulations, but may also be organized according to more or less stable scales of values.

However, there also exist values of yield linked with the costs and profits of functioning. It may be argued that economic and even praxeological values are all more or less hedged around by legal norms: an individual who does not pay his debts is proceeded against and another who steals, i.e. practises what Sageret jocularly described as the most economical form of conduct (*maximum* of profit with *minimum* of expense), is punished by law. But the definition of the frontiers between what is permitted and what is forbidden is one thing and the actual determination of a value by a norm is another. Economic value obeys its own laws which legal rules cannot determine and which do not in themselves lay down any obligation (a norm is recognizable by an obligation which may be honoured or violated, as opposed to a causal determinism which constrains but does not 'oblige' in this normative sense). Economic value is of course inseparable from all kinds of values of finality and normative values; likewise, the internal praxeology of an organism or of individual behaviour (that 'economy' which certain psychologists hold to be the principle of elementary affectivity) is connected with many questions of structure. But the general problems of cost and profit are quite distinct from those raised by other forms of evaluation and cannot but lead to multiple interdisciplinary research, as the numerous and increasingly widespread applications of the theory of games demonstrate.

Thirdly, in all spheres of human behaviour there are systems of *meanings* or messages, the essential part of which is studied by linguistics within the collective system of language. But while language has played a rôle of the first importance in human societies by the oral and written transmission of values and rules of every kind, it does not constitute the only system of signs and especially of symbols belonging to the mechanism of messages. Without mentioning the language of animals (bees, etc.), which raises all kinds of problems of comparison, it should be remembered that the appearance of representation in individual development is not due to language alone but to a much wider semeiotic function also including symbolic play, mental image, drawing and all forms of deferred and interiorized imitation (the latter constituting the transitional term between sensori-motor functions and representational functions). Further, language – which constitutes, so to speak, a system of messages to the power of one – is accompanied in collective life by systems to the power of two, such as myths, which are simultaneously symbols and semantic characters carried by verbal or graphic sign-vehicles. Thus general semeiology gives rise to interdisciplinary problems of the broadest kind.

## II. STRUCTURES AND RULES (OR NORMS)

Having posed the problems in their most general forms in sections 1 to 4, let us now try to go into the details of common mechanisms by following the plan provided by the distinction between rules, values and signs.

## 5. *Concepts of structures*

One of the most general trends of avant-garde movements in all the human sciences is structuralism, which is taking the place of atomistic attitudes or 'holistic' explanations (emergent wholes).

The method intended to master problems of wholes – which at first seems to be the most rational and rewarding because it corresponds to the most elementary intellectual operations (those of assembling or adding together) – consists in explaining the complex by the simple, in other words in reducing phenomena to atomistic elements the sum of the properties of which is supposed to represent the whole which has to be interpreted. Such atomistic methods of posing problems eventually lead to the laws of the structure as such being forgotten or distorted. They have by no means disappeared from the field of human sciences and may be found for example in psychology in associationist theories of learning (school of Hull, etc.). Generally speaking authors frequently revert to these types of additive constructions when a certain empiricism or a mistrust of theories which they consider premature impels them towards what they believe to be greater respect for directly observable facts.

The second trend which can be observed in a number of separate disciplines is one which, in the face of complex systems, consists in stressing the characteristics of 'wholeness' peculiar to these systems, while considering that wholeness to be directly 'emergent' from the assembly of elements and as imposing itself upon them, by structuring them, as a result of this constraint of the 'whole'; above all, it consists in considering the whole to be self-explanatory by the mere fact of its description. Two examples of such an attitude may be given, one corresponding to certain current psychological trends and the other connected with a sociological school which is now extinct. The first example is that of certain adherents of 'Gestalt' psychology which was principally the product of experimental studies on perception but was extended by W. Köhler and M. Wertheimer into the field of intelligence and by K. Lewin into that of affectivity and social psychology. According to some of these authors we proceed in all fields from an awareness of wholes preceding any analysis of the elements, these wholes being due to effects of 'fields' which determine the forms by quasi-physical principles of equilibrium (minimum action, etc.); the whole being distinct from the sum of its parts, Gestalts then obey laws of composition which are non-additive but are of qualitative predominance (*Prägnauz*) (the 'best' forms prevail by reason of their regularity, their simplicity, their symmetry, etc.). The prevalent opinion today is that this method offers good descriptions but not explanations and that, if one advances from perceptive or motive Gestalts to forms of intelligence, these latter constitute systems which are additive but which nevertheless involve laws as being complete systems (which puts the problem in terms of algebraic structures or systems of transformations and no longer in terms of Gestalts).

In an entirely different field, Durkheim's sociology proceeded in a similar manner by seeing in the social whole a new totality emerging on a higher scale from the assembly of individuals and reacting upon them by imposing on them a variety of 'constraints'. It is interesting to note that this school, whose twofold merit was to emphasize with particular vigour the specificity of sociology as distinct from psychology and to supply an impressive body of specialized work, likewise died a natural death for the lack of a relational structuralism which might have supplied some laws of composition or construction instead of referring unremittingly to a totality conceived as ready-made.

The third position, then, is that of structuralism, but interpreted as relational, that is to say as positing systems of interactions or transformations as the primary reality and hence subordinating elements from the outset to the relations surrounding them and, reciprocally, conceiving the whole as the product of the composition of these formative interactions. It is of great interest, from our interdisciplinary point of view, to note that this trend – which is increasingly evident in the human sciences[11] – is still more general and manifests itself just as clearly in mathematics and biology. In mathematics the Bourbaki movement has led to breaking down the frontiers between the traditional branches in order to identify certain general structures regardless of their content and to draw, by combinations or differentiations, the details of particular structures from three mother-structures. And although this process of fusion has today been replaced by analysis of 'categories' (classes of elements with their functions), that is again a form of relational structuralism, but one which comes closer to the effective construction characteristic of the work of mathematicians. In biology 'organicism' similarly represents a *tertium* between pseudo-mechanistic atomism and the emergent wholes of vitalism, and the most convinced theoretician of organicism has created a movement of 'general theory of systems' with interdisciplinary aims as regards, *inter alia*, the field of psychology

(Bertalanffy has been influenced by Gestalt theory but goes considerably beyond it).

Having said this, there exists a whole range of possible 'structures' spread over three directions, and our first problem is to understand the relation between them (the first of these directions corresponds to what we called completed structures in section 3 and the other two to structures in process of formation or not closed):

1. Algebraic and topological structures, including logical models since logic is a particular case of general algebra (for example, the ordinary logic of propositions is based on Boolean algebra). Thus in ethnology Lévi-Strauss reduces kinship relations to group or lattice structures, etc. In intelligence theory we have tried to describe intellectual operations the formation of which can be followed in the course of individual development by defining overall structures in the form of elementary algebraic structures or *'groupements'* (akin to groupoids) and then, at the level of pre-adolescence and adolescence, of lattices and groups of assembled quaternities. Structuralist linguistics likewise has recourse to algebraic structures (monoids, etc.) and the same is true of econometrics (linear and non-linear programmes).

2. Cybernetic circuits which describe systems of regulations and whose use is essential in psychophysiology and in learning mechanisms. Ashby, the designer of the famous 'homeostat' which enables problems to be solved by a process of balancing, has recently supplied in his *Introduction to Cybernetics* a model of regulation whose feedback actions are themselves determined by an imputation table of the games theory type. This model, which he regards as one of the most general and the simplest to be made biologically, shows a possible link between psychological and praxeological or even economic regulations (see section 13).

3. Stochastic models used in econometrics, demography and often in psychology. But whereas chance plays a constant role in human events and therefore requires to be treated on its own, it is never pure in the sense that the reaction to the fortuitous, whether favourable or unfavourable, is in varying degrees an active reaction, which brings us back to regulations. Thus this type 3 results from a complication of 2, as type 2 is of 1 (remembering that the operation is a 'perfect' regulation with pre-correction of errors).

Thus structuralist research gives rise to at least three major interdisciplinary problems (without semantic correspondence with these three types of structure but in relation to them as a whole):

*a.* A problem of comparison of structures according to their spheres of application. It is not by chance, for example, that structures of perception ('good forms', perceptual constancy regarding size, etc., systematic errors or 'illusions', etc.) refer to models of regulations which are more or less close, or applicable, to an assumed whole, and that structures of intelligence at various levels of equilibrium relate to algebraic models; the reason is that the latter involve a logic, whereas perceptual structures, despite their partial (but only partial, while Gestalt theory postulated direct identifications) isomorphisms with the former, contain a possibility of systematic deformation (or 'illusions') which from the algebraic viewpoint constitute 'non-compensated transformations'. The same goes for the unquestionable advantage to be found in looking among social phenomena for those which do or do not relate to a particular type of structure, which amounts in the end to delimiting what is amenable to logic and what is a matter of guesswork and readjustment.

In this connexion attempts can be made (and we have tried to do this in genetic psychology) to establish 'partial isomorphisms' to facilitate such comparisons between structures, in particular by specific fields. Such a concept has no meaning from a purely formal point of view, which requires that an isomorphism must be total or not exist at all; after all, anything is partially isomorphic with anything else. But the method acquires concrete and genetic meaning if two preliminary conditions are set for such research: 1) that one can determine the transformations which are necessary in order to pass from one structure to an adjacent one, and especially, 2) that one can show, genetically or historically, that these transformations are effectively achieved in certain situations or are sufficiently probable (by direct affiliation or by collateral kinship, the common trunk from which the branches diverge being specified).

*b.* This leads us to the second of the major intradisciplinary or interdisciplinary problems raised by structuralist research. Whereas the explanation of wholes by atomistic methods leads to a geneticism without structures and the theory of emergent wholes leads to a structuralism without genesis (which is also partially true of Gestalt theories or of any irreducible social view in sociology), the central problem of structuralism in the biological and human sciences is that of reconciling structure and genesis, since every structure involves a genesis and every genesis must be conceived as the (strictly formative) transition of an initial structure to a final structure. In other words, the fundamental problem is that of the filiation of structures, and the triad of algebraic, cybernetic and stochastic structures immediately raises the question of the possibilities of transition from one of these categories to the others.

There is above all the problem of relations between cybernetic and algebraic structures, and in this connexion genetic psychology supplies some highly significant indications. Between the elementary levels where cognitive conduct proceeds by trial-and-error or immediate perceptive intuitions (two forms implying regulations in the sense of cybernetic circuits) and those levels where, towards 7–8 or 12–15 years, algebraic structures recognisable by the strict co-ordination of 'operations' are constituted (as actions which are directed inwards, reversible and related to overall structures with their laws of composition), one finds all the intermediary stages in the form of pre-operational representations still involving simple regulations but tending towards a form of operation. From this one may conclude that operation constitutes the limiting stage of regulation in the sense that the latter, being at first a correction of error as the result of action and later a correction of action as anticipating its possible deviations, finally becomes pre-correction of error, which is the function of operational deduction: feedback is then promoted to the rank of an inverse operation and the system by its composition alone ensures all the possible compensations. Although it is not possible at present to say whether this process is peculiar to the field under consideration or can be more generally applied to others, we may conceive of similar processes in the spheres of the sociology of knowledge, sociology of law and sociology of moral facts, and possibly also in structuralist linguistics.[12]

*c.* The third major problem which arises in comparative studies is that of the nature of the structures arrived at, i.e. whether they constitute simple 'models' in the service of theoreticians or whether they should be considered as inherent to the reality under study, in other words as structures of the subject or subjects themselves. This question is fundamental, because in the eyes of authors critical of structuralism the latter is merely a language or a computing instrument which refers to the observer's logic but not to the subject. This problem is often raised even in psychology, where experimentation is relatively easy and where one can in certain cases be fairly sure that structure reaches down to the underlying explanatory principle of phenomena, in a sense which recalls what the philosophers call the 'essence', but with the addition of an undeniable deductive power. But in disciplines where experimentation is difficult, even in the broadest sense as in econometrics, experts often stress the divergence they see between the mathematical 'model' and the 'experimental design', a model without sufficient relationship with the concrete being no more than a play of mathematical relations, whereas a model which adopts the details of the experimental design can claim the status of a 'real' structure. It goes without saying that in most situations the models used in the human sciences are placed, still more than physical and even biological models, halfway between the 'model' and the 'structure', in other words between the theoretical design partially related to the observer's decisions and the actual organization of the behaviours to be explained.

*Note.* – Lastly, we should say a few words about a problem allied to the preceding one which we were advised to include in the list of topics covering all the sciences of man, namely that of what some have ventured to call the 'empirical analysis of causality'. Two questions should be carefully distinguished here, that of causal explanation in general and that of functional dependence between observable facts which can be identified either by dissociation of factors in experimental research or by analysis of multi-variabilities in non-experimental research (in economics and sociology, cf. the works of Blalock, Lazarsfeld, etc.). The second of these questions does indeed concern all the human sciences, but from an essentially methodological point of view, without leading, properly speaking, to the discovery of new common mechanisms unless by further refining the concept of functional dependence as opposed to simple correlations. On the other hand, the problem of causal explanation in general brings out the latent conflict which will doubtless exist for a long time yet between the partisans of a positivism wedded to observables and those authors who seek to identify, beneath those observables, 'structures' capable of accounting for their variations. It goes without saying that problems of causality are reduced, if such structures exist, to the lattices formation, their internal transformations and their self-adjustment; seen in this light, the search for functional dependence is only a stage towards the discovery of structural mechanisms, and the analysis of function could not be pursued to any length without arriving sooner or later at these mechanisms. As to which of these two fundamental lines of approach will eventually prevail, it is not for us to say. For the moment we should merely note the rather striking convergences becoming apparent between schools of thought which may be described by the very general name of genetic structuralism in psychological research on development, in the study of 'generative grammars' in linguistics, and in certain analyses, outwardly very different, in economics and Marxist-inspired sociology.

## 6. *Systems of Rules*

The third problem we have raised (under *c*) often finds a possible solution in the following form: when following the formation of a structure one observes on its completion some modifications in the subject's behaviour which are difficult to explain otherwise than by that completion itself, in other words by the 'closure' of the structure. These are fundamental facts which are translated in the consciousness[13] of the subject by feelings of obligation or of 'normative necessity' and in his behaviour by obedience to 'rules'. Let us recall that according to the habitual, if not general, terminology of experts in the study of 'normative facts'[14] a rule is recognized by the fact that it imposes an obligation but can be either violated or respected, contrary to a causal 'law' or determination which suffers no exceptions unless it be by reason of contingency variations due to a mixture of causes.

An example should explain this rôle of the closure of structures. A child of 4 or 5 years is generally unable to deduce that $A < C$ if he has noted separately that $A < B$ and then that $B < C$ (but without having seen $A$ and $C$ together). Moreover, he is unable to construct a seriation of slightly differentiated objects $A < B < C < D$ ... or manages to do so only by groping. On the other hand when he later achieves a flawless construct consisting in the successive placing of the smallest of the remaining elements (hence comprehension of the fact that an element $E$ is simultaneously greater than the preceding elements, $E > D, C$, etc., and smaller than the following elements, $E < F, G$, etc.), he resolves by so doing the problem of transitivity and will no longer judge $A < C$ as undecidable or simply probable, but as necessary ('it's got to be', etc.) if he has seen that $A < B$ and $B < C$. This feeling of logical necessity, difficult to evaluate like all states of consciousness, will be translated in behaviour by the use and recognition of transitivity.

Many other examples could be quoted in other fields of individual development, such as the emergence of a sense of justice as a highly imperative norm succeeding a morality of obedience at the age where relations of reciprocity are structured outside or in opposition to relations of subordination. In the historical development of societies it seems clear likewise that democratic ideals have gained currency as a function of changes in structures, etc.

Thus the study of rules or normative facts constitutes an important sector of the study of structures, the more so as it provides a link between structuralism and the actual behaviour of subjects. Moreover, such rules are observed in all the fields covered by the human sciences; even in demography it is impossible, for example, to dissociate the birth rate from a variety of moral and legal rules. Where Durkheim saw the process of 'constraints' as the most general social fact, he was expressing this common characteristic of various social behaviours, namely, that they are accompanied by rules.

There arise out of this a certain number of interdisciplinary problems which are as yet far from being resolved, but in respect of which a twofold trend can be observed: they are raised in every field and they are treated by means of bilateral connexions. We may distinguish three such problems:

*a.* The first question is to establish whether rules or obligations are necessarily of a social nature, that is to say whether they presuppose an interaction between at least two individuals, or whether they may be of an individual or endogenous character. The queston is merely a sub-division of the more general question whether all 'real' or natural structures (as opposed to exclusively theoretical 'models') are translated in the behaviour according to rules.

To this more general question one might be tempted to reply immediately in the negative, since there exist, for example, perceptive structures whose social component is nil or very small[15] and which are not accompanied by 'rules' in the normative sense. However, they are translated by 'predominances' ('good form' wins over an irregular form, etc.), and in the opinion of certain authors there are many intermediate stages between predominance and logical necessity, which would raise the question of relations between the normative and the 'normal', not in the sense of a simple dominant frequency but of the state of equilibrium (achieved, moreover, by self-regulation, which implies possible new connexions between the 'regulable' and the 'rule').

The question therefore is far from simple. The dominant trends would seem to be the following: on the one hand there is increasingly general doubt as to the existence of 'innate' rules such as a logic or a morality transmitted through hereditary channels.[16] Natural logical operations begin to occur only very gradually (on an average hardly before 7 or 8 years in developed societies) in accordance with a constant sequential order but without that fixed regularity in age levels which would bear witness to internal or nervous maturation. They are certainly drawn from the most general forms of co-ordination of actions, but these are collective as much as individual actions, so that they appear to be the result of a progressive balancing of a psycho-sociological kind, far more than as biologically inherited (in other words the human brain contains no hereditary programming, as would be the case if logico-mathematical behaviours constituted something in the nature of instincts; instead it shows a hereditary functioning the utilization of which allows both collective life and the setting up of general co-ordination from which these structures obtain their point of departure). Moral obligations, as J. M. Baldwin, P. Bovet and Freud have shown, are linked in their formation with inter-individual interactions, etc.

Moreover it appears increasingly probable that if every balanced structure imposes not only regularities but also a certain predominance due to its own regulations, and if every system of regulations involves, by the very fact of its successes or failures, an obligatory distinction between the normal and the abnormal (concepts peculiar to living matter and devoid of meaning in physico-chemistry), there nevertheless exists a kind of limiting point which both separates and unites regulations and operations (see section 5). This point of transition might well in many cases be that between the individual and the inter-individual.

*b.* A second general problem which follows on from what we have just said is that of types of obligations or rules. Logical necessity is translated into coherent operations capable of constituting deductive structures, but there exists a large number of obligations and rules without intrinsic consistency, arising essentially from constraints of a more or less contingent or momentary kind, the extreme case being that of the rules of spelling whose arbitrary nature is sufficiently demonstrated by history. Even independently from the questions raised under *a*, it is evident therefore that not every obligation extends into possible 'operations' in the limited sense in which we have adopted this term (section 5), but that a certain number of systems of rules do not go beyond the level of structures of regulations.

The second general problem raised by systems of rules is thus to construct, by means of interdisciplinary comparisons, a hierarchy of varieties of structures, starting with operational structures of various forms and ending with those which are based on regulations, likewise of various forms and involving a greater or lesser degree of chance.

*c.* The third great problem raised by systems of rules is that of interference between rules belonging to different fields. This problem, some examples of which we shall presently discuss, occurs in two forms. First there is the question of effective intersections of structures leading to interferences between rules: for example, a legal system is a body of rules *sui generis*, that is to say irreducible to moral or logical rules; but objectively it involves all kinds of interferences with those other two systems by the mere fact that it must not contradict either of them (which may be easier in one case than in another).[17] But there are also intersections due to the subject's realization of the structure, this realization perhaps being adequate but partial or distortive as a result of various subjective influences. Thus the usual grammar of teachers is nothing other than a very incomplete and in part distortive realization of linguistic structures and generally interferes with obligations of the quasi-moral type.

## 7. *Examples of interferences in the field of logical structures*

The case of logical structures is a good example of how impossible it is today to isolate a form of research which yet is very distinct and possesses every characteristic that might have made of it a kind of absolute, secure from interdisciplinary contacts. Formal logic is at present perhaps the most exact of disciplines in terms of the rigour of its demonstrations. It can be placed at the starting point of mathematics, so much so that one might hesitate to include it among the sciences of man and that those responsible for the organization of the present series have not included it among the disciplines selected for study. Above all, logic, using as it does an axiomatic or 'formalizing' method, ignores the psychological 'subject' as a matter of principle, having become a 'logic without subject' so that the attributes it has mapped out for itself forbid it even to inquire whether 'subjects without logic' even exist.

Yet the internal evolution of logic itself as well as the external evolution of branches outside its field compel us to note the existence of numerous centrifugal trends which inevitably give rise to problems of interdisciplinary connexions.

The first of these trends arose from the discovery by K. Goedel in 1931 of the limits of formalization. In a series of celebrated theorems Goedel showed that it is impossible for a theory of a certain richness (e.g. elementary as opposed to transfinite arithmetic) to demonstrate its own non-contradiction solely by its own means and by logical means weaker than those it implies; in this way it must of necessity arrive at certain undecidable propositions, and in order to decide these it is necessary to resort to 'stronger' means (e.g. transfinite arithmetic). In other words logic is no longer an edifice resting on its base but a construct whose consistency depends on higher levels which are never completed because each in turn has need of the next. But as soon as there is a construct we must ask: a construct of what and by whom? And if there are limits to formalization we must ask why, to which J. Ladrière, for instance, replies by invoking the impossibility for the subject to embrace in a single actual field the totality of its possible operations (which in fact is an appeal to psychology to produce an epistemology of logic; see below).

Another and equally remarkable internal trend is the concern shown by certain logicians for establishing a connexion between formal logic and certain systems of norms or rules used by subjects collectively. We have already quoted (section 4) works like those by Weinberger, etc., which apply formal logic to connexions between norms posed in the imperative. But mention should be made especially of the important work of the Belgian logician Ch. Perelman in the field of argumentation. Perelman sets out to study from a logical point of view the many situations where a partner seeks to act upon another not through sentiment or extrinsic arguments of authority, etc., that is to say not through those sophisms which have so wrongly been grouped under the name of 'logic of sentiments' (for the true logic of sentiments is morality, with which Perelman is beginning to concern himself), but through an argumentation which is logically coherent although directed and organized so as to convince. A vast body of works has appeared on this subject[18] among which we find in particular a study by L. Apostel on the presuppositions of such a theory and more particularly on the relations between logical operations and the general co-ordination of actions (Apostel shows in this respect the kinship between Perelman's analyses and the writer's own research on the development of logical structures proceeding from action). Starting from the theory of argumentation, Perelman has naturally been led to study the logic of legal structures, and a very active collaboration on this issue between jurists and logicians has been established under his direction and has already yielded a number of studies.

A third trend common to certain logicians consists in taking an interest in psychology, not of course in order to find in it the internal foundations of logic (which would mean going from the fact to the norm, or 'psychologism', as little valid as the inverse movement or 'logicism') but with a view to its general epistemology. If it is the nature of logic to be a construct, it becomes difficult to interpret it epistemologically as a simple language and moreover a strictly tautological one as logical positivism proposes. That is why logicians who no longer believe this thesis or have never believed it are turning in the direction of psychological or psycho-social construction of structures. It should be noted, however, that this is not simply a formalization of 'natural' thought or logic, which is of limited interest (except in situations where it develops specific techniques such as that of argumentation, which has been analysed by Perelman): first because natural logic is generally poor compared with the richness of axiomatics, but especially because it constitutes only a highly imperfect realization of the underlying structures. What these logicians are seeking is therefore less an analysis of the consciousness of subjects than a study of structures, in their filiations and formations, which then makes it possible to show the stages whereby one arrives, starting with elementary behaviours, at the algebraic structures of logic itself (Boolean algebra and network, etc.). This is the subject studied by the logicians working at the International Centre of Genetic epistemology in Geneva: L. Apostel, S. Papert, J. B. Grize, C. Nowinski, etc.

One of the reasons why the problem of the epistemology of logic thus forms a bridge between logic and genetic psychology, is that the latter has for years gone out to meet problems of this kind. For it is impossible to study the development of the intelligence from the first years of childhood to adolescence or to the adult state without coming up against a certain number of findings which fall within the sphere of logic. The first of these findings is that even in the pre-language stage there exist, at the level of sensori-motor action patterns, certain structures of interlocking, order, correspondence, etc., which prefigure logic and display its links with the general co-ordination of action. Later we find that by a process of successive balancings the common operations of classification, seriation, correspondence or intersection come to constitute (towards 7–8 years) formalizable structures halfway between 'groups' and 'networks', which we have called 'groupings'. We find above all that at a third stage (11–12 years) these groupings are co-ordinated simultaneously in a quaternality group and a network of interpropositional connections. For interdisciplinary research it is of interest to note that this 'group' of propositional transformations, widely studied by logicians since 1950, was discovered in genetic psychology before it was analysed in its logistic formalization.

Relations between logic and economics are of two kinds, thanks to the theory of games. On the one hand the logician may take an interest in games theory as in any other logico-mathematical procedure in order to establish its axiomatics. On the other hand, however, induction (in other words the full range of inferences applied to a field of experience where contingency intervenes) is a 'game' between the experimenter and nature, and it is possible to conceive of a theory of induction based on strategies and decisions. Since several authors regard deduction as an extreme case of induction, we thus see the connexion between logic as a whole and epistemology. There is no need to recall that this epistemology of logic can *a fortiori* be placed in relation with cybernetics by a double movement similar to that just referred to, which we may cite with T. Greniewski, an expert in connexions between logic and cybernetics.

As to exchanges between logic and linguistics, we shall come to them when discussing the latter.

## 8. *Systems of non-deducible norms: sociology of law, etc.; customs and habit patterns*

Independently of the specific questions of legal logic which have been discussed, there exists a major problem the importance of which has found expression in several contemporary trends in a variety of disciplines, namely that of the general structure of systems of norms. From this viewpoint of overall structures, which is becoming increasingly dominant, it is by no means sufficient to know that a particular legal reasoning can be put in logical form; this does not alter the fact that a legal system in its total form in the sense employed by H. Kelsen (from the 'fundamental norm' and the constitution to individualized norms such as all court judgements, diplomas, etc.) is at the same time very close to a logical system and very different from it.

The analogy is that in both cases there exists a construct of normative values achieved by means of actions or operations, and that these results are valid depending on a series of transitive implications. If such and such axioms are accepted, then such and such theorems $T_1$ follow which lead to such and such other theorems $T_2$, etc., according to a series of implications placed in hierarchical order. Thus if a constitution is accepted, then parliament has the right to enact laws $L$ which are valid by virtue of the constitutional norm; then the government has a right to take a decision $D$ which is valid by virtue of the law $L$; then such and such an office has the right to settle an individual case $C$ in a valid manner by virtue of the governmental decree $D$, etc. This succession of normative constructions (each norm being at the same time the application of the previous one and the creation of the next one) is readily comparable to a series of implications, and Kelsen explicitly defines this implicative relationship under the term of 'imputation' (central or peripheral depending on whether it qualifies the subjects of law or the implications alone).

The great difference however is that if one knows the content of axioms, one can deduce the succeeding theorems: they were not, of course, tautologically pre-formed within the axioms, since these axioms are independent one from another, but the new combinations obtained are 'necessary' (they could not have been other than they are by virtue of the given operations). In the legal system, on the other hand, one merely knows that parliament cannot violate the constitution, but within this framework it votes what it likes; in other words the constructive operations take place in a valid fashion as a function of transitive and necessary imputations, but their results remain contingent because they are not determined by the form of these operations, only their validities being so determined to the extent that they are not in contradiction with norms of a superior category.

In other words there exist normative structures whose actual form determines their content and which for this reason can be described as formal, and others whose form does not determine their content. The former, which can give rise to 'pure' deductive disciplines (pure logic and mathematics) nevertheless concern all human behaviour, since economic exchanges could not proceed beyond the barter stage if everyone did not accept the fact that twice two makes four. There is therefore some advantage in making a comparison of structures and systems of rules from the standpoint of these relations between form and content, and it will be seen at once that such comparative analyses can be carried out only by means of close interdisciplinary collaboration.

The study of moral facts offers another example of such problems and it is not pure chance that this subject has attracted the interest of sociologists, psychologists, certain logicians, jurists,[19] experts in the sociology of law and an appreciable number of economists (utilitarian explanations of moral facts are essentially the product of schools of thought built up by Anglo-Saxon economists). The French economist J. Rueff, in a highly stimulating study on moral facts, has raised the problem of the formalization of different moralities, using the significant terms 'Euclidian' and 'non-Euclidian' moralities to bring out the differences in postulates associated with moralities observable and widespread in the social group. By following the psychogenetic development of moral rules in the child and adolescent, the writer has been led to distinguish in that development two clearly distinct forms of structures depending on whether the source of the norms is to be found in obedience to persons who are the object of unilateral respect or whether it relates to a system of reciprocity or mutual respect (that being, in particular, the source of concepts of justice which are acquired independently and often to the detriment of the morality of obedience). From the point of view which concerns us here, the former of these moralities clearly belongs to those structures whose form does not determine their content, while in the latter we do observe an effect of form upon content. The writer was accordingly able to try to formalize the second of these two systems, in which it is not difficult to find analogies with those logical operations which are involved in an inter-individual co-operation of a cognitive nature. Thus the generality of such problems becomes evident at once.

Indeed these problems are so general that they can be found in all those aspects of social life which Durkheim described under the common term of 'constraints' and within which we must distinguish at least two poles: that of norms imposed by an authority or by custom, which place an obligation on the individual without his participating in their creation, and that of norms resulting from a collaboration of a kind in which the partners contribute to the formation of the norm which places an obligation upon them. It will be seen at once that the latter case is oriented in the direction of systems whose form determines their content to varying degrees.

The problems crystallize in particular around the question (always a central one) of relations between custom or habit and obligation or rule. When Thurnwald in a famous phrase laid down that 'recognised constraint transforms custom into law' he was raising a much more general problem than that of the birth of law in tribal societies, and one which is still under study today: how does one move from a structure which is simply regular or balanced to a system of rules or norms? In the sociology of law the formula we have quoted emphasizes with great truth that custom does not suffice so long as there has been no 'recognition'. Similarly in the field of moral facts neither habit nor example are sufficient, so long as a certain relation of 'respect' or recognition of a value connected with the person has not been established (and no longer connected merely with transpersonal functions or services, as in the legal sphere). But in the field of intellectual operations where, as we have just seen, the very form of the norms determines their content, although logic is certainly a morality of the exchange of thought and of cognitive co-operation, a certain coefficient of internal necessity attaches to any deduction based on a balanced operational structure, as though the transition from action to reversible operation were sufficient to engender the regulated structure which governs cognitive common production as well as individual constructs. Lastly, in the sphere of patterns of habit and perception peculiar to the individual alone, although no normative necessity is involved, there nevertheless exist phenomena of predominance due to an internal balance where there is no longer any question of norms but where we are nevertheless faced with an attenuated form of that necessity which dominates in the higher varieties of balance.

Hence the trend which we discern in this line of research would lead to the acceptance of the fact that the transition of structures into rules presupposes two conditions. The preliminary condition is a condition of balance: the structure becomes a rule only if it closes back on itself in a sufficiently balanced form which expresses itself in predominances of different kinds if that balance is due to regulations, and by intrinsic necessity if it is operational. The second condition appears with inter-individual relations and is once again a matter of forms of balance, but in this case forms which are relative to these collective situations: their regulations or the operations which derive from them are then expressed by those different states of consciousness which lead from trans-personal recognition or from respect for persons to various forms of obligation properly speaking.

## 9. *Diachronic and synchronic problems in the field of norms*

It is well-known that linguistics, beginning with the works of F. de Saussure, has proceeded to dissociate diachronic studies, or studies of history and evolution of language, from synchronic considerations connected with the balance of language as an existing system in a state of relative independence from its past. We also know the extent to which economic crises can modify the state of values and so dissociate them from their previous history. On the contrary, it is in the nature of rules or norms to introduce compulsory conservation, which is why their function is of such great importance in the life of societies and individuals. The norm is therefore by its very nature the essential instrument of connexion between the diachronic and the synchronic.

The fact remains that structures and rules develop, that they were formed little by little, and that even in the case of progressively acquired stability new structures or norms can modify the meaning of preceding ones to a more or less deep extent, even if they do not replace them. We are thus confronted with a new major problem of interdisciplinary comparison, that of the uniformity or variety of relations between diachronic and synchronic factors depending on different types of structures or norms.[20]

Taking logical norms first, these may appear to constitute the prototype of unchangeable structures since a variety of philosophers from Plato to Husserl have linked them with Ideas, *a priori* forms or eternal or at least timeless fundamentals. A. Comte, one of the precursors or founders of scientific sociology, described the development of fundamental concepts in his *Law of the Three States* (whose value we are not called upon to discuss here), but maintained that this development concerned only the content of human reason whilst its forms, in other words the actual processes of reasoning or 'natural logic', remained invariable. A trend which is fairly general today, owing to the history of sciences and techniques; to work on comparative sociology and on genetic psychology; and especially to the evolutionist viewpoints which are now dominant in ethology and zoopsychology, leads us to think on the contrary that reason was built up by stages and continues to evolve, not without reason or reasons but in such a manner that not only is the evidence transformed but even that which appears logically demonstrated or rigorous at a given stage may subsequently appear doubtful and may give rise to considerably greater degrees of rigour.

On the other hand, if reason evolves, the progressive constructs to which it may give rise constitute an extremely remarkable type of development in the sense that the previous structures are not set aside or destroyed but are integrated in the subsequent ones as specific cases valid in a certain sector or at a certain scale of approximation. The same is not true of the experimental sciences, starting with physics where a theory can be contradicted by another or retain only a limited degree of truth. But in the field of logico-mathematical structures no structure which has been demonstrated as valid at a moment in history is subsequently abandoned, the error consisting merely in believing it to be unique and in that sense necessary, whereas later it becomes the sub-structure of a richer and broader whole. From the point of view of relations between the diachronic and the synchronic we thus have here an exceptional situation in which the existing equilibrium appears as the product of a historical process of more or less continuous balancing (crises or momentary imbalances being no more than crises of growth or break-throughs to new problems).

If we compare this situation with that of a system of legal norms, the contrast is striking. A well-made system of such norms does, of course, provide for its own modification in the sense that as soon as a constitution exists, and at every stage of normative construction provided and implied by it, there is a possibility of revision or modification. In a certain sense therefore there is continuity in normative creation, and in this respect we find here the connexion between the diachronic and the synchronic which is peculiar to systems of rules as opposed to systems of non-normative values or signs. Yet the situation is quite different from that which exists in the case of rational norms. In the first place there is nothing to prevent the new norm from replacing and contradicting the one which is abolished; this does not create any break in the transitive succession of valid 'imputations', but it does create a discontinuity in the actual content of the norms. Secondly, the relative continuity of which we have been speaking remains subordinate to the stability of the political régime; in the event of a revolution, the entire system is abolished for the benefit of a new one unrelated to the old.

In the field of moral norms continuity is doubtless greater, but the problem of relations between diachronic and synchronic factors nevertheless arises in very different terms from those of logical norms. When Durkheim, who tended to subordinate the synchronic entirely to history, explained the prohibition of incest in developed societies by the exogamy of tribal organizations, he was forgetting to explain why so many other rules likewise attributed to totemism have not been perpetuated in our time.

There is no point in piling up examples to show that this is a field of interdisciplinary research of considerable general importance. In the last analysis the question comes down to this: to what degree is contemporary man dependent on his history? A superficial answer based on what has just been demonstrated would be to maintain that historical factors are vitally important precisely because they are timeless and are, like rational norms, a matter of invariables which history uncovers but does not create or explain; while the great historic changes which introduce continuities between certain systems of norms and the preceding ones would, by this reasoning, stress the importance of synchronic rebalancings rather than of continuous constructive processes. In reality there is a history of events or of visible and in part contingent manifestations, and there is also the history of the underlying dynamism or of processes of elaboration and development. We are becoming increasingly aware that organic development is far more than a history of events or a succession of phenomena, but is a matter of progressive structuration or organization whose qualitative stages are subordinate to an increasing integration. That is why the history of civilization is becoming more and more an interdisciplinary task within which the history of science and technology, economic history, diachronic sociology, etc., have to analyse concurrently the innumerable facets of the same transformations. But it is also why history is explicative even in what appear to be its timeless invariables, because they have become such only as a result of constructive processes and balancings which have to be reconstituted and which, by varying from one field to another, mutually illuminate one another both in their differences and in their common mechanisms.

III. FUNCTIONING AND VALUES

In all the sciences of life and of man there has always been opposition between so-called functionalist trends and structuralist trends. In biology Lamarck maintained long ago that 'the function creates the organ', whereas the neo-Darwinian theory of fortuitous variations and of selection after the event tended to deprive Lamarck's formulation of any significant content; but the contemporary views; according to which the phenotype is a 'response' of the genome to the tensions of the environment; tend to go beyond both terms of the alternative by creating a new synthesis. In the psychological and social disciplines the conflict is equally general between a functionalism some of whose adherents see in the 'structures underlying the observables' no more than simple abstractions created by theoreticians, and a structuralism some of whose adepts regard the functional aspects of behaviour as secondary characteristics without explicative meaning. It is therefore a major interdisciplinary problem to identify the common mechanisms which might be capable of co-ordinating functions and structures in all human behaviour. This problem naturally leads to that of utility or values as objective or subjective indices of functioning, and also to the problem of the possibility of a general theory of values based not on *a priori* reflection but on possible convergences that may emerge from mutual connexions between research in all our fields.

### 10. *Functioning and functions. Affectivity and praxeology*

We must first ask ourselves whether the conflicts between functionalism and structuralism do not in part stem from too narrow a conception of structures which emphasises only their characteristics of totality and internal transformations but overlooks their essential property of self-adjustment. For if this property is neglected, the structure takes on a static aspect which devalorizes functioning, thus giving the impression that with structure one has established a kind of permanent 'entity' related to the unchangeable properties of the human spirit or of society in general. Hence the scepticism of functionalists vis-à-vis such a hypothesis, which can in effect lead to anti-functionalism.

But if one distinguishes between formal or formalized structures, whose adjustment is due to the axioms conferred upon them by theoreticians, and real structures which exist independently from theory, it is necessary to ask how structures are conserved and how they act, which comes down to raising the question of their functioning. Their self-adjustment can in some cases be assured by rules or norms, as we have seen under ii, but then these rules already represent a function, that of maintaining the integrity of the structure by a system of constraints or obligations. On the other hand it may be that the structure is not completed; in its formative stages its self-adjustment will of course as yet imply not a system of rules but a self-regulation whose functioning may involve multiple variants. In particular it may happen that a structure is not capable of 'closure' but depends on continual exchanges with the exterior (see section 3). It is in such situations that functions are distinct from structures and that functionalist analysis becomes necessary to such a point that its partisans sometimes forget that it is difficult to conceive of functions without organs or overall structure.

Thus the problem of accurately defining the relations between structures and functions is a general one in the human sciences and requires constant interdisciplinary help. In this connexion we should recall how K. Lewin, whose social psychology is the product of Gestaltist structuralism, came to describe the actual needs in that language and how W. Köhler, his teacher, wrote a whole work on 'the place of values in a world of facts'. Let us also recall how T. Parsons called his method in sociology 'structural-functional', considering structure to be the stable arrangement of the elements of a social system unaffected by fluctuations imposed from outside, and function as occurring in the adaptations of structure to situations exterior to it.[21] In economics, J. Tinbergen sees structure as 'the consideration of not immediately observable characteristics concerning the manner in which the economy reacts to certain changes'. These characteristics, expressed in terms of econometric coefficients, give on the one hand an architectural picture of the economy but, on the other hand, indicate the ways in which it reacts to certain variations; thus we find once again that structure is accompanied by functions because it is capable of 'reactions'.

If the structuralism of Lévi-Strauss leads to a certain devalorization of functionalism, that is essentially due to the fact that genetic and historical factors are, so to speak, bound to be overlooked when one is studying societies whose past is unknown and doubtless lost without recall. On the other hand it is interesting to note that the 'neo-functionalism' of young American sociologists such as A. W. Gouldner and P. M. Blau is by no means closed to structuralist perspectives. Thus both these authors endeavour to clarify the relations between sub-systems and system, and to re-examine the classical problem of social stratification, basing their analyses, however, on the central notion of 'reciprocity' in the one case and on that of elementary 'exchanges' in the other. It seems clear that such viewpoints in no way conflict (quite the reverse) with what we described in section 5 as relational structuralism, their specific nature being that they do not proceed from totalities in order to come down to constituent relations but from the latter in order to illuminate the functioning of sub-systems.

Generally speaking one may (cf. section 3) consider functioning as the structuring activity whose structure constitutes the result or the organized event. In the case of a completed structure functioning is identical with those transformations which are real among all those which are possible, and which characterize the system as such. As to function, the term can be used to designate the particular rôle played by a specific transformation relative to that entire set of transformations (the two meanings, biological and mathematical,[22] of the word 'function' then tend to become interchangeable). But in the case of a structure in process of formation or of development, or generally not 'closed', where for that reason self-adjustment so far consists only in regulations and where exchanges are open to the exterior, functioning is formative and not merely transformative and functions correspond to utilities (or values) of various kinds depending on the rôles of conservation, reinforcement or perturbation which the functioning of sub-systems may play in relation to the total system, or vice versa.

It is from this viewpoint, among others, that an interdisciplinary model such as that of the theory of 'general systems' is of particular value (a system being defined as a complex of elements in non-contingent interaction). In his works on scientific thought A. N. Whitehead already supported the notion that interpretations usually denounced as being 'mechanical' could not deal exhaustively with the analysis of the real and that the concepts of organism or organization have specific characteristics which ought to be used. Proceeding from biology (but also from a Gestalt-oriented psychological view), L. von Bertalanffy studied this problem by seeking to derive from this 'organicism' certain general models whose interest is not merely biological (theory of 'open' systems and their specific thermodynamics) but also extends to a certain number of the human sciences insofar as it is possible to generalize the notions of homeostasis (*inter alia* for the theory of needs), differentiation, stratification, etc.[23] Experiments in the mathematical analysis of such structures having an 'organized complexity', with which A. Rapoport and others have been associated, rapidly showed the convergence between some of these anticipations and N. Wiener's[24] cybernetics, especially in the field of 'equifinality' (arrival at final states which are relatively independent of initial conditions). But the central problem remains that of relations between sub-systems and the total system when (and this is the general case of structures not yet reducible to algebraic forms) the composition of the whole is not additive or linear.

To return to functions, utility or values, it therefore seems evident that to the extent that the structures under consideration are in process of development (or of regression), questions of functioning are at the heart of the problems. Any genetic process which results in structures undoubtedly consists of balancings alternating with imbalances followed by rebalancing (which may succeed or fail), since human beings never remain passive but constantly pursue some aim or react to perturbations by active compensations consisting in regulations. It follows from this that every action proceeds from a need which is connected with the system as a whole and that values likewise dependent on the system as a whole are attached to every action and to every situation favourable or unfavourable to its execution. In the sphere of cognitive structures, where needs and values are relative to the activities of comprehension and invention, such a model makes it possible to explain simultaneously the psychological progression of stages of mental development and the logical nature of the structures thus achieved (since regulations lead to operations and balancing leads to their reversibility; see section 7). This cognitive development is already a social as much as a psychological or even a biological one, since the operations of the individual are indissociable from inter-individual co-operation (in the most etymological sense of the word). Thus the model seems to be partly open to generalization in the social field as a whole (we shall return to this issue in section 14), but only on condition that consideration is given to needs and values of whatever nature, not only in their cognitive forms.

In this connexion reference should undoubtedly be made to a specific type of research which may be called 'praxeology' (cf. *Main Trends*, vol. 3) and which is a theory, essentially interdisciplinary, of behaviours as relations between means and ends from the viewpoint of yield as well as of choice. Certain authors have tried to reduce all economics to this question, e.g. L. Robbins who speaks of 'relations between rare (or limited) ends and means with alternative uses' (*An Essay on the Significance of Economic Science*, 1932) and L. von Mises; but although economics does in certain respects constitute a sector of praxeology, it is a sector which involves many other factors and a complexity of social inter-actions and which cannot be reduced to these simpler relations already present in exchanges between the individual subject (or the organism itself) and his physical and inter-individual surroundings.

In order to understand the very general scope of these praxeological analyses and their effects on the theory of values as a whole, it is necessary to start by recalling the present state of trends as regards relations between affective life and cognitive functions.

A highly significant fact likely to concern all the human sciences strikes us from the outset, namely the surprising difficulty met in trying to characterize affective life in relation to cognitive functions (insofar as these relate to structures) and especially of defining their inter-relations in the actual functioning of behaviour. This fact immediately gives rise to the general problem as to whether values, or at least some values, are determined by structures and in what sense; whether these values or some of them (on the contrary or in turn) modify structures and which ones; or whether values and structures are two aspects – indissociable but so to speak parallel – of all behaviours whatever they may be. It is immediately evident that the problem goes well beyond the sphere of psychology, for whereas praxeology, as the 'general theory of effective action' (E. Slucki as early as 1926, T. Kotarbinski 1955, O. Lange, etc.) invokes a 'principle of rationality' (*maximum* effects with a *minimum* of means), that principle concerns affective values as much as cognitive structures.

In psychology the general trend today is to distinguish in any behaviour a structure which corresponds to its cognitive aspect and an 'energetic' element which characterizes its affective aspect. But what is the meaning of this somewhat metaphorical term 'energetic'? Freud, who was reared in the atmosphere of the 'energetic' school (as opposed to atomism) of the physicist E. Mach, himself sometimes a psychologist, saw instinct as a reserve of energies whose 'charges' are stored in certain representations of objects which by that fact become desirable or attractive. The terms 'investment' or cathexis have become current in this connexion. K. Lewin visualizes behaviour as a function of a total field (subject and objects) in the Gestalt manner, the structure of this field corresponding to perceptions, acts of intelligence, etc., while its dynamics determine functioning and eventually attribute positive or negative values to the objects (characteristics of attraction or repulsion, barriers, etc.). But the problem which remains is that an operational mechanism unquestionably involves a dynamic and that it is necessary to distinguish within it the structure of transformations as such and what makes them possible in their desirability, interest, speed, etc.; and this second aspect brings us back to an 'energetic'. P. Janet distinguishes in all behaviour a primary action or relation between subject and object, which corresponds to (cognitive) structures, and a secondary action which regulates the former as to its activations (interest, effort, etc., on the positive side or fatigue, depression, etc., on the negative side) and to its terminations (rejoicing in the case of success, sadness in that of failure). This suggests that elementary affective life expresses behaviour adjustments, but what kinds of adjustments (for these may be structural or cognitive)? Janet explicitly puts forward the hypothesis of a reserve of physiological forces which are stored, used up or reconstituted in accordance with variable rhythms, and suggests that it is these forces which affectivity regulates in accordance with a 'behaviour economy' co-ordinating gains and losses of energy. Going on to generalize at the inter-individual level, Janet analyses sympathy and antipathy from this point of view, people for whom one feels sympathy being energy sources or excitants and those for whom one feels antipathy being tiring or 'costly'.

This brings us to a first problem: does affectivity as 'investment' or as a series of regulations depending on gains and losses actually modify structures or does it merely ensure their functioning in terms of energy? Some authors believe the former, arguing that the systematic defect of 'investment' characteristic of schizophrenics who are not interested in reality leads to a schematic and pathologically formal type of thought, while the 'over-investments' of paranoiacs lead to loss of reason (delusions of grandeur, etc.). Other authors (including the writer) think that a child with a lively interest in arithmetic and another suffering from multiple complexes regarding itself will both recognize that two and two make four and not three or five, because activity makes structures function by accelerating or retarding their formation but without modifying them; and that the behaviour difficulty in a schizophrenic or a paranoiac can simultaneously affect structures and their affective functioning according to a dynamic which always involves both aspects at once.[25] But of course it remains possible that a distinction should be made between structures whose form determines the content (logico-mathematical structures) and those whose content depends on a variety of values, although in a 'value judgement' the form (or judgement) is structural and therefore cognitive and the content is relative to affectivity precisely as a value.

The second problem, however, is even more important and concerns all the human disciplines to a still greater extent, namely that of the multiplicity of values or of their reduction to their energetic 'economic' (in the praxeological sense) dimension alone. When the economist speaks of production, exchange, consumption, reserves or investments, etc., we see clearly enough that these terms recur in exactly the same form in every field, including that of the affectivity of infants before all language (in terms of expenditure or recovery of energies, 'investing' in objects or people, etc.); but it remains to be known whether the meanings involved are always comparable. And it is impossible to attempt a classification without immediately finding that it applies to all the sciences of man (certainly including linguistics, if only because F. de Saussure drew his inspiration from economics and because the 'affective language' described by Ch. Bally gave rise to a theory of values by the sociologist G. Vaucher).

As an introduction to this classification (in section 11) we should first recall that in the sphere of individual as well as inter-individual values there exists a fundamental duality which recurs everywhere,[26] namely that of values of finality (or instrumental values, i.e. means and ends) and values of yield (costs and benefits) which are inseparable but clearly distinct from one another. In the individual sphere this distinction is based on the double meaning of the word interest. On the one hand all behaviour is dictated by interest in the general qualitative sense, in that it pursues an end which has value because it is desired, and this end can be entirely disinterested (in the second meaning of the term) although it is of great interest in the first sense. On the other hand interest is an energy adjustment which releases the available forces (Claparède and Janet), that is to say increases the yield, and from this second point of view a behaviour is called 'interested' if it is intended to increase the yields from the viewpoint of the subject's ego. By playing on these two meanings of the term while refusing to distinguish between them, utilitarianism sought to explain altruism by selfishness under the pretext that all behaviour is interested – which is false since behaviour is always directed by interest in the first meaning of the term and can therefore be, as we have just shown, disinterested and interested at the same time. This sophism is sufficient in itself to justify the two types of values. Furthermore, when Janet explains sympathy and antipathy in terms of values of yield he is right in a large number of cases, e.g. when one chooses a travelling or table companion, but it is possible to love an extremely tiring person, and one does not always marry a woman for the sole reason that she is 'economical' in the sense that she will not prove very wearying. We may even consider that 'investments' of affective charges which occur in love are a function of a common scale of values, of twin production projects in the broadest sense and even of values which are highly disinterested although they involve interest (in the other sense of the term) to an exceptional degree.

## 11. *Classification of values*

The gist of the foregoing is that praxeology is everywhere, but nowhere by itself. It is impossible to accomplish a moral act or to perform a logical operation without expenditure of energy, which is a matter of values of yield, whereas the behaviours studied by economic science may have no matter what intrinsic finality and whereas concepts of production and consumption are necessarily related to structures accompanied by their own values or finalities. It is therefore evident that all the sciences of man lead to the search for a classification of values.

1. One must first justify the first dichotomy suggested by the psychology of affectivity, which recurs everywhere. Values of *finality*, or instrumental values, bring together those which are by their very quality related to structures, in other words which correspond to the needs of qualitatively differentiated elements, with a view to the production or conservation of structures. That is not to say that values and structures are identical; a structure exists on the strength of its own laws, which can be described in terms of algebra (including logic) or topology without reference to speeds, forces or energies as working capacities;

and this same structure can be desirable and indeed must be so for the subject to take an interest in it; this then presupposes an intervention of affective charges or 'investments', etc., i.e. of energy. From this second point of view a further distinction has to be drawn between the choice of elements to be invested (values of finality) and the quantities involved. Values of *yield* are then precisely relative to this quantitative aspect if we admit by definition that a yield is distinguished from a qualitative result by reason of the quantity produced or expended (quantity of energy in the case of intra-individual 'economy' or technical production, conventional or accountable quantity in the case of commercial exchanges).

2. Values of finality may give rise to a second dichotomy. Structures to which these values are attached can be translated by rules which are to a greater or lesser extent capable of logical expression, or which may remain at the level of simple regulations. In the former case we may speak of *normative* values to the extent that the value is influenced or actually determined by the norm, whereas in the case of spontaneous and free exchanges we may speak of *non-normative* values. As to the former, one may once more wonder whether value and norm or structure are identical. But, once again, that is not the case since the norm comprises its (cognitive) structure on the one hand and its value on the other, the latter being as usual related to affectivity; we have seen (in section 8) that a moral norm is accepted only as a function of specific feelings of respect which are a valorization of the person issuing instructions or of partners in a relationship of reciprocity. A legal norm, on the other hand, is valorized only as a function of an attitude of 'recognition' which is the valorization of a custom or of a trans-personal relationship.

Non-normative values of finality extend to many diverse fields. In the first place, they grow from individual interests to inter-individual sympathies and to those in numerable exchanges which make up everyday social life, whether these be exchanges of information, economically non-quantified services of all kinds, politics, courtesy, etc. In addition they also include those valorizations which occur in symbolic expression by means of gestures, clothes, words, etc., since systems of symbols or signs include – besides their strictly semeiotic laws – a body of values which tend either to reinforce or diminish expressivity, as Bally has shown with regard to what he called 'affective language'.

3. Lastly, values of yield accompany all the foregoing but give rise to specific valorizations which express themselves both in the internal energetic praxeology of action (cf. in section 10 the conceptions of P. Janet) and in inter-individual economics dealt with by economic science. In both cases it is striking to note the predominant importance of quantification as compared with the qualitative nature of values of finality. In other words, as soon as there is a question of yield, what counts is no longer the quality of the objective judged in relation to a differentiated need (that need itself expressing either a gap or a momentary imbalance in a structure which has to be completed or re-balanced), but the quantum of the result obtained in relation to the expenditure required in order to obtain it.

## 12. *Regulations and operations relative to valorizations of finality*

The concept of finality has a bearing on all the human sciences since there is scarcely a form of human behaviour that does not involve intention. Yet we know well enough that finalism has given rise to many difficulties and presented a problem in biology until the formulation of present-day solutions which seem to offer satisfaction, at least on the level of principles. Three phases may be distinguished in this connexion.

During the first phase, which was of psychomorphic origin, finality seemed to carry its explanation within itself as being a causal principle. Aristotle, who attributed finality to all physical movement as well as to living processes, separated 'final causes' from 'efficient causes', as though the existence of an aim entailed *ipso facto* the possibility of attaining it, which presupposes either a consciousness (within which the aim corresponds to an existing representation) or an effect of the future upon the present.

In the second phase, the unintelligible nature of this final cause led to the concept of finality being broken down into its components, a causal explanation being sought for each. Thus the concept of direction found its explanation in processes of achieving balance; that of anticipation in the utilization of previous information; that of functional utility in the hierarchic nature of organization, etc. As to the central concept of adaptation, efforts were made to reduce it to two concepts of fortuitous variation and of selection after the event, which replaces finality by a set of tentative efforts (at the phyletic as well as the individual level) directed from the outside through successes and failures.

The present phase, which is marked by very comparable schools of thought in the sphere of the human sciences, results from the conjunction of three kinds of influences. In the first place, while finalism has never supplied satisfactory explanations, it has always excelled at denouncing the inadequacies of over-simplified mechanistics. To explain the eye by hazard and selection is all very well if one has plenty of time, but if it requires more generations than the age of the earth will allow, as has been calculated on the basis of, if anything, favourable postulates, it is best to search in other directions. Secondly, analysis of phenomena – which always begins in an atomistic mood – leads in all spheres of life to the unveiling of regulations; after the discovery of physiological (homeostasis) and embryogenetic regulations, the notion was abandoned that the genome is an aggregate of independent particles, and it was sought instead to establish the existence of co-adaptations, regulator genes, 'responses', etc. Thirdly and particularly, these organistic trends, which originated in part independently from mathematical models, were found to converge with one of the fundamental discoveries of our age, that of the mechanisms of self-regulation or self-direction studied by cybernetics. This was rapidly followed by the realization of the possibility of supplying a causal interpretation of finalized processes and of finding 'mechanical equivalents of finality' or, as one says today, a 'teleonomy' without teleology.

It is in this context, needless to say, that a certain number of trends are at present evolving towards an analysis of regulations in the field of functioning and values as well as in that of structures. But it should also be noted that in the human sciences as in all others, but in the biological disciplines in particular, efforts are directed first of all – and rightly so – towards the two extreme ends of the range of phenomena, for it is the comparison between these extremes which offers the best chance of understanding the whole range of mechanisms involved. This pendulum action is particularly evident in economics. After limiting itself in many cases to micro-economics, economic science – following the intuitions of Quesnay and especially the conceptions of Marx – struck out on the path of macro-economics, and the same is true of the differently oriented work of Keynes. However, with operational research and econometrics there has been a new trend to re-establish the micro-economic approach. In sociology, where the degree of precision is naturally much smaller owing to the complexity of the problems involved, we observe an instructive process of shuttling back and forth between macro-sociology and micro-sociology. In the sphere of values of finality it goes without saying that a double approach is needed, since while global exchanges, etc., show irreducible aspects depending on overall mechanisms, it is only in the sphere of elementary reactions and exchanges that we may hope to witness the birth of valorizations and in certain cases to determine their connexions with psycho-biological functioning.

In the sphere of normative values it goes without saying that moral facts are studied principally from their psychological and micro-sociological angles, especially as there exists no adequate method at the higher levels except where societies are of limited dimensions, like those studied in cultural anthropology. But even in fields where consideration of wholes would appear to be necessary, as for instance in the sociology of law (since positive law is linked with the life of the entire State down to its most individualized applications), there exists a movement which has attempted the study of, as it were, micro-juridical process-es. Thus, marginally to codified law, or at the point where it begins, Petrazycki has analysed attributive imperative relations such as that the right of one part-ner corresponds to an obligation for the other. This relation, which is distin-guished from the moral relation (although less so than Petrazycki believes, since while it is true that the moral obligation of a subject $B$ confers no right upon his 'neighbour' $C$, it nevertheless results from the right which $A$ or $C$ had to issue instructions to him or to enter into reciprocity with him), is also clearly distinguished from codified or structured legal order and thus charac-terizes a kind of spontaneous or deontological juridical view which is interesting from the viewpoint of mechanisms of valorization.

In the sphere of non-normative qualitative values the writer has attempted to analyse the mechanism of the exchange which determines valorization and its relations with normative consolidations.[27] In any relationship between two in-dividuals $A$ and $B$, what is done by one of them, say $rA$, is evaluated by the other according to a satisfaction $sB$ – positive or negative – which may be conserved in the form of a kind of debt or psychological gratitude $tB$, the latter for that reason constituting a credit or a valorization $vA$ for $A$ (process naturally following a sequence $rB$, $sA$, $tA$ and $vB$). A large number of circumstances may of course prevent a balance in the form of equivalences $r = s = t = v$: over- and under-evaluation, forgetfulness, ingratitude, using up of credit, inflation, etc., and especially discordances between momentary or durable individual scales of values. Nevertheless the formula can be used to describe the most varied situations: sympathy between two individuals as based on a common scale and profitable exchanges; a person's reputation with or without inflation; real or fictitious exchanges of services which affect credit in micro-politics, etc. Although without practical interest, this type of analysis helps to establish two small theoretical assumptions.

One is the often striking analogy between such processes of qualitative exchange and certain elementary economic or praxeological laws. In the first place it goes without saying that evaluations and reputations $s$ and $v$ are rather closely subject to the law of supply and demand: the same average talent gives rise to entirely different estimations in a small town, where it enjoys a certain 'rarity value', and in a more dense environment. Furthermore one finds here, despite the absence of quantification, an equivalent of Gresham's law ('bad money drives good money out') in situations of crisis or imbalance where new scales of values take the place of others and where reputations are readily inflated but fragile, etc.

Secondly, it is easy to see that the conservation of the virtual values $t$ and $v$ (as opposed to the real or existing values $r$ and $s$) remains partially contingent so long as the exchange remains non-normative, whereas any course of action launched in accordance with an obligation leads to new relationships imposed by this structure (just as in economic exchange, cash sales involve few legal relations while credit sales presuppose a greater measure of protection). Thus the value $t$ is eroded of its own accord through forgetfulness or ingratitude, etc., whereas the intervention of a moral sense of reciprocity leads towards conservation (the French word '*reconnaissance*' means both spontaneous gratitude and the fact of recognizing a debt or an obligation). The transition from spontaneity to normative reciprocity is marked by a new type of exchange where there is no longer simply an approximate correspondence between services and satisfactions, etc., but substitution of points of view, that is to say access to decentred or disinterested attitudes.

The above is only a small example of possible analysis. Many others can be found in the current, highly lively work of American neo-functionalism already referred to (Gouldner, Blau, etc.). Hence the sphere of qualitative values represents a fairly large potential area of comparative research, even including transition from regulations to reversible operations. We have already seen (in section 5) that this transition is under study in the structural sphere proper (cognitive regulations and operations). There is no reason why the same should not apply to the sphere of values, in terms of attractions or 'investments' of affective charges, reciprocities and exchanges, in isomorphism with what is observed in the case of structural regulations and operations. A first striking fact in this connexion is the logical form assumed by scales of values – seriations, genealogical trees, etc. – and authors like Goblot have attempted a 'logic of values'.

But above all there exists a system of operations bearing not on the knowledge of structures, but on the regulation of available forces, and the theory of games has given it status under the name of 'decision': this is the will, the explanation of which has never ceased to create problems and difficulties for psychologists. Since W. James it has been generally agreed that the will is not a simple tendency capable of isolation, unless confused with effort or intention. The will intervenes when there is a conflict between a tendency which is judged inferior and is momentarily the stronger (a specific desire, etc.) and a tendency which is judged to be superior but is initially the weaker (a duty, etc.); the act of will consists in reinforcing the latter tendency until it overcomes the former. A. Binet concluded from this that there is a need for an additional force, and Ch. Blondel suggested that this force derived from collective imperatives (a questionable solution since if such imperatives are sufficient to determine an action there is no further need for the will, and if they are not sufficient the problem remains intact). The solution would seem to be the following: a tendency is neither strong nor weak in itself but only in relation to the context; so long as that context is merely a matter of fluctuating adjustments bound up with the perceptive existing situation, the lower tendency is likely to prevail; if the will is interpreted as a reversible operation or as the extreme stage of normal energy adjustments, the act of will can then be seen to consist in deflecting the subject's concentration from the existing situation ('decentration') so as to allow a return to the permanent values of his scale. Hence having a will means being in possession of a scale of values sufficiently resistant to be referred to in the course of conflicts. The analogy with intellectual operations (section 5) is evident.[28]

13. *Cybernetic circuits and economic adjustments*

Values of finality play a very general part in all fields of the human sciences, but unfortunately they are not always measurable for that reason. Values of yield, on the other hand, are measurable by their very nature, and since economic science is concerned with both types of values simultaneously, it is in this field that the meaning of these two kinds of common mechanisms, active in all human behaviour, can be most readily appreciated.

Generally speaking every value is the expression of the functioning of the structure and every functioning is a flow subject to regulations, that term being taken in its broadest sense to cover both the spontaneous processes of balancing and intentional and systematic regulations such as economic regulations resulting, for example, from a policy of stabilization or one of growth. Our problem in this section is therefore to seek to identify the most general models of regulations applicable to all spheres of values, and for this purpose to examine the manner in which economists use the notions of cybernetic circuits to master the complex systems of interactions with which they are confronted. This is not to say, of course, that loop circuits (or feedbacks) are the result of the work of economists; quite on the contrary, economists are only now beginning to take an interest in the operational content of the theory of servo-mechanisms,[29] not merely as a result of intellectual inertia but owing to the difficulty of adapting the complexity of experimental measurements to that theory. But the example of economics is of particular interest, in the first place because of the convergence between these models and classical concepts such as that of the economic circuit and, secondly, because the generalized nature of economic mechanisms is already becoming apparent, some of their central aspects recurring in the fields of biology, psychology and even of linguistics.

The advantage of loop systems is that they confer a clearly defined status on some of the innumerable situations in which concepts of interaction and circular causality have to be substituted for the concept of a linear causal sequence. In physics the principle of action and reaction, the existence of many systems which retain their balance by compensation of the various equivalent efforts which they allow, and Le Châtelier's law (or the law of equilibrium displacements in the direction opposite to that of the initial disturbance) show the impossibility of reducing certain forms of causality to a linear sequence pattern. In biology the very fact of organization and its conservation through successive adjustments involving on each occasion a set of gains and losses makes the consideration of loop systems more and more indispensable, and even in the case of apparently simple effects of an environment on an organism (phenotypical modifications or selection with genetic effects) it is increasingly believed that the organism chooses and modifies its environment as much as it depends upon it, which suggests the relevance of cybernetic circuits. In the sphere of the human sciences, where interactions are always accompanied by automatic or more or less intentional regulations, the notion of circuits is even more obviously applicable and it is becoming increasingly apparent that even the general pattern $S-R$ (stimulus−reaction) is itself circular in nature, for a subject reacts to a stimulus only if he is sensitized to it, and he is sensitized to it only as a function of the pattern which determines the response, without it being possible to interpret the latter in turn independently of the habitual stimuli.

In the field of economics, which offers the advantage of allowing extensive measurements, a certain number of notions which have gained currency prepared the way for cybernetic models. Such a notion, for instance, is the somewhat intuitive one, but one essential to economic thought, of a 'variable which is self-influencing by means of other variables dependent upon it'. Such also is the notion of the 'economic circuit', for instance in the relations between production, consumption and investment, which constitute numerous cases of circular causality. Such too are the notions of multiplicator and accelerator, frequently used by economists, which can furnish examples of simple transformations in a loop system.

Let us, for the sake of concreteness, give an elementary example (taken from L. Solari) of the translation in feedbacks of an economic circuit. Let us suppose that this model refers to a closed national economy (without exchanges with other countries) and let us assume only three variables, as follows: $Y(t) =$ national product, $C(t) =$ global consumption and $I(t) =$ global investment. These variables are continuous functions of time $(t)$; they represent monetary flows within an interval $t$, $t + dt$. We then obtain the accounting relationship:

$$Y(t) = I(t) + C(t)$$

which may be completed, e.g. by the introduction of the two behaviour laws

$$C(t) = c.Y(t) \text{ and } I(t) = v\,\frac{dY(t)}{dt}$$

$c$ and $v$ being respectively the marginal propensity towards consumption and the investment coefficient.

The former is a function of consumption of the most common type. The second law translates globally the reactions to the investment decisions of economic agents faced with variations in the national income: we have here, in its simplest form, the well-known phenomenon of the accelerator which 'repercusses', as regards investment, the variations in the national income. This elementary dynamic model may then be reduced to the differential equation

$$\frac{I-c}{v} = \frac{I}{Y(t)}\,\frac{dY(t)}{dt}$$

the immediate solution of which, taking account of the initial condition $Y(o) = Y_0$, is $Y(t) = Y_0 o^{pt}$ with, for the sake of simplification,

$$p = \frac{I-c}{v} = \frac{S}{V},$$

where $S$ represents the marginal propensity to save. The rate of growth $p$, normally positive, is therefore proportional to the propensity to save and inversely proportional to the investment coefficient. The model can then be represented by the following diagram in which the circles represent variables and the parallelograms represent the transformations undergone by them (in the direction of the arrows):

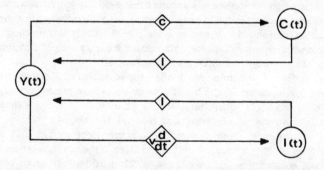

Feedbacks may be recognized in the two loops of the diagram. The first translates the 'multiplicator effect': $Y(t)$ is self-influencing through the agency of $C(t)$. The second translates the 'accelerator effect': $Y(t)$ is self-influencing through the agency of $I(t)$. Both effects are additive.[30]

The method of which the foregoing is a concrete example offers two advantages, one from the viewpoint of economic research itself and the other in that it supplies a representation of mechanisms common to all the life and human sciences (not only because loop systems are found in them all but also because circles of production, consumption and investment recur in all fields of values of finality as well as values of yield).

From the viewpoint of economic science (which, we repeat, can serve as an example because, *inter alia*, of its infinite possibilities of measurement), patterns such as the one we have just examined make it possible to carry out a logical and causal analysis of the interactions involved, and there is nothing to prevent this analysis from being extended to the consideration of more complex transfers or of new feedbacks. In particular it is possible to add to the model we have shown, which already relates to regulations in the general sense of the term, a regulatory feedback in the limited economic sense (policy of stabilization, which here would in fact be a policy of growth): it would be enough to introduce a new variable $G(t)$, such that $Y(t) \rightarrow G(t) \rightarrow Y(t)$, making it possible to modify the rate of growth $p$ by the nature of the transfer achieved[31] (the model would of course have to be expanded to take account of delayed variations, which play an essential motivating rôle in economic regulations).[32]

The general significance of such models is considerable; in fact they represent one of the most important common mechanisms in the field of values and even in that of the build-up of structures.[33]

As for values, that is to say, as we have seen ( section 10), the rôle of the affective life in general, it is clear that the loops connecting production with consumption or investment recur in the most widely different situations: all production, i.e. all constructive action, is reinforced or held back by its own results, i.e. by the consumer actions to which it gives rise; on the other hand it leads to new affective 'investments' which reinforce the initial action or supplement it with others. Thus we have here a very general mechanism from which the economic models we have just examined differ only by their specific social characteristics and by the remarkable degree of quantification to which they lend themselves.

As to the build-up of structures, this is closely linked to what we have just called production in the general sense of constructive actions. From this it follows that in all fields a structure which finally acquires a well-regulated or logico-mathematical nature (e.g. a 'group' structure) starts with a phase of simple adjustment, i.e. of construction by trial and error whose corrections are effected by means of feedbacks analogous to those described. Later, once the structure has been sufficiently balanced, the play of reversible operations takes the place of the initial regulations (as we have seen in section 5): correction as a function of the results alone is then replaced by an anticipatory pre-correction of the actions in progress, and the loop system thus arrives at a system of direct and reverse operations whose regulation is now identical with its constructive activity (the values initially involved being thereby promoted to the rank of normative values).

14. *Synchronic and diachronic problems in the sphere of functions and values*

We have seen (in section 9) that the normative structure achieves a condition of equilibrium (with, or course, variable degrees of stability depending on the relations between form and content: see section 8) as a function of a process of development which itself constitutes at all stages a balancing in the sense of a process of self-regulation. This self-regulation is to varying degrees inherent in the actual production of the structure in that there are no constructive mechanisms on the one hand and no corrective mechanisms on the other hand or after the event, but that progressive organization – in which construction consists – is at the same time a regulating one and therefore proceeds by balancing. We shall see (in section 18) that a system of meanings, in contrast to this, shows a maximum of disjunction between the history of the sign-vehicles, on which their present meaning depends only in part, and the synchronic balance of the system which is relatively independent from diachrony. The system of functions, utility or values lies halfway between these two extreme situations, and it is highly interesting in the study of common mechanisms to note that this intermediate position, from the viewpoint of relations between synchrony and diachrony, recurs in all disciplines having an important functionalist dimension, from biology to economics by way of psychology and sociology, in other words wherever a distinction has to be drawn between present utility and historical filiation.

In the field of economic history, for instance, this intermediate situation shows the two following characteristics. On the one hand one frequently finds a bipolarity between the endeavour to explain some set of present (or in any manner synchronic) facts by its previous development and the reverse approach which seeks to interpret a set of historical events by general mechanisms considered to be 'timeless' and related to the laws of balance. But on the other hand one finds in Marx and his followers a methodology which sets out to overcome this duality of historical and supra-historical factors dialectically by resorting to what might be called today a genetic structuralism in the sociological, psychological and even biological fields.

As regards the duality of interpretations found in authors not influenced by Marx, everyone agrees in assuming that major economic structures are explained by their history, whereas events related to current situations (such as the cost of certain foodstuffs in the 13th or 16th centuries, referred to in section 2) are interpreted in the light of theories on the determination of prices which lead to these mechanisms being considered 'timeless and necessary', by no means because these prices do not vary but because their variations in historical curves which are irregular in detail are held to depend on laws of balance recurring over a fairly wide range of social situations.

By contrast, the originality of Marx's approach consisted in seeking to overcome this conflict between structures and fundamental laws by regarding neither as 'eternal' and subordinating both to an overall dynamic force. As regards structures, Marx of course emphasized the temporary or historically transitory nature of capitalism, whose laws were regarded as permanent by the classical economists. But with regard to the laws of functioning, Marx made the very basic point that these laws frequently begin to operate 'in the pure state' at the stage of maturity of the system; thus a study of function at the terminal stages would lead to an understanding of the history of the structure from which this functioning proceeds. Hence the fundamental observation (in the *Critique of Political Economy*) revealing the links between Marx's methodology and biological problems: 'The anatomy of man is the key to the anatomy of the ape', which is to say that final states illuminate the process from which they result as much as that process is necessary to the development of those states.

But this reference to biology, which stresses the very general nature of the problem of relations between structural diachrony and functional synchrony, leads us to enquire into the particular status of concepts of function, utility or values in relation to structural development and, finally, to reflect once more on the reasons why it is difficult to treat history as a nomothetic discipline.

In the field of biology an organ can change its function without that change resulting from the previous history of the structure concerned: to borrow a classical example, the fact that the swim-bladder of the *Dipneusti* now serves as their lung is not due to the general historical factors which ensured the evolution of the Invertebrates into Fishes, but results from unforeseeable changes in the environment. It is therefore doubtful whether it will ever be possible to create a deductive model of the history of life which would supply the details of all known transformations, whereas we may be permitted to hope for an 'organicist' model (see section 10) which would account both for the general characteristics peculiar to living structures and for the major functions common to all or almost all organisms, such as assimilation, respiration (except for viruses), etc. But these 'functional invariables' are of variable content and are thus differentiated in the course of their history, and that history, like all genuine history, constitutes an inextricable mixture of deducible and contingent structurations: whereas reactions to the contingent consist in regulations or rebalancings which are intelligible after the event, the sequence of their succession is nevertheless unforeseeable, and this makes the present functions of a sub-structure relatively independent of its previous development.

The same applies in part to the sphere of human history, despite the corrections implied in man's twofold specificity, of having created a culture which incessantly enriches itself because it is socially transmitted and of having a reflexive intelligence which makes it possible to multiply rational behaviours (despite their obvious limits in the common consciousness). It follows that although certain historians would like to give nomothetic status to their discipline by means of interdisciplinary fusion of the history of science and technology, of economic, cultural and political history and of diachronic sociology, etc., the laws of development or functioning that could be derived therefrom might nevertheless differ considerably, depending on the types of structure envisaged and, consequently, on the varieties of possible relations between structures on the one hand and of functions, utility or values on the other.

Were we to assume that we could adopt as one methodological ideal that of genetic structuralism, which indeed seems to be common to many disciplines, the fact nevertheless remains that the distinction between structures capable of 'closure' and structures as yet incomplete or destined to remain open for all time imposes a series of differentiations which express themselves in particular in the need to recognize several varieties of values depending on whether they are normative or non-normative, etc. (sections 10 and 11). C. Nowinski, an expert in Marxist methodology, has pointed out, for instance, that 'the kinship of methods as between genetic psychology and Marx's theory is sometimes surprising. There remains, however, an important difference. For Piaget the notion of balance as the central mechanism and necessary mainspring of the process of development remains characteristic, although each state of equilibrium succeeds the previous one by reason of the imbalances which engender it. For Marx, conversely, the central mechanism of development is the continuous destruction of equilibrium, with all the methodological consequences which result'.[34] The reason for this difference is strikingly obvious: the development of intelligence culminates in completed structures in which functions and values are entirely subject to the normative laws of internal structural transformations, which means that such development is directed by equilibrations or self-regulations leading to the final balance; but biological, economic, political, etc., structures, being constantly open, cannot – because of the absence of closure – involve such complete integration of function in the structural mechanism, whence the historical role of imbalances which can actually lead to integrations of structures.

This situation, peculiar to structures incapable of closure, explains the relative independence of values connected with synchronic balance from the diachronic formation of the corresponding structure. This is observed in the case of certain crises (provided they are neither accidents of growth nor durable disintegrations) where one may find abrupt modifications of economic, political, or social values (reputation, personal credit) or of the affective values of an individual. And it also accounts for the difficulty of characterizing sequential stages (i.e. stages occurring in a necessary order of succession) in the social sphere and the relatively small success of the 'stages' which Rostow believed he had discovered in the processes of economic growth (from take-off to maturity). The general problem in this respect consists in distinguishing a sequence of transformations without organized internal development from a development with sequential stages involving in particular what Waddington in embryology called 'homeorhesis' (automatic return to the necessary trajectory in the case of a deviation imposed from outside).

Such facts seem to demonstrate that functions and values are the more dependent on history and diachronic explanation as they are better subordinated to the corresponding structures. A system of values, on the other hand, obeys laws of equilibrium or of present regulations which are the less dependent on the preceding stages the less those values are normative, that is to say the less they are conditioned by the structure alone and depend on exchanges whose external conditions may vary. In other terms, the balance of these values does not in such a case represent the final stage of a progressive diachronic balancing but remains the synchronic expression of situations in part independent of development; in this case there occurs only a succession of rebalancings whose laws may be constant but whose contents vary, in part contingently and in part cyclically.

## IV. MEANINGS AND THEIR SYSTEMS

Every structure of rule and every value has meanings, just as every system of signs has a structure and values. Nevertheless, the relationship of *signifiant* to *signifié* differs in kind from that of desirability (value) or the structural (or normative) subordination of one element to the whole to which it belongs. And this relationship of meaning is again extremely general in scope, so that interdisciplinary problems are as important in this sphere as in the previous ones.

## 15. *Biological signalling and semeiotic function*

Reactions triggered by indices or signals are to be found at almost all levels of animal behaviour, ranging all the way from the simple sense-reaction of protoplasm in the unicellulars to the sense-reaction of the nervous system or its responses to meaningful messages. Moreover this type of meaning, linked to signals or indices, is the only observable one in children until around 12 to 16 months (sensori-motor levels) and it remains at work in regard to perceptions and motor-conditioning throughout life. It was therefore necessary to begin by recalling the rôle of this initial system of signalling.[35]

Index is the name given to a *signifiant* which is not differentiated from its *signifié* (except by its signalling function), in that it constitutes a part, an aspect or a causal result of that *signifié*: a branch protruding over a wall is an index of the presence of a tree, and the tracks of a hare are the index of its recent passage. A signal (like the sound of the bell which triggers the salivary reflex in Pavlov's dog) is only an index, unless there is attached to it a conventional or social significance (telephone ringing, etc.), in which case it is a 'sign'.

In some higher primates and in man (from the second year) there appears a set of *signifiants* which are differentiated from their *signifiés* in that they no longer simply belong to the designated object or event, but are produced by the subject (individual or collective) with a view to evoking or representing those *signifiés*, even in the absence of any immediate perceptive stimulus on their part: such are symbols and signs, and semeiotic (or often, symbolic) function is the term given to that capacity of evocation by differentiated *signifiants* which then makes possible the construction of the image or thought. But there are two levels still to be distinguished in these semeiotic instruments, although in the normal child they all appear more or less at the same time (except as a rule in drawing).

The first level is that of symbols, as the term is used by de Saussure in contradistinction to signs: these are the *signifiants* 'motivated' by a resemblance or some analogy with their *signifiés*. They appear in the child in completely spontaneous fashion with symbolic (or fictional) play, deferred imitation, the mental image (or interiorized imitation) and the graphic image. The initial feature of these symbols is that the individual subject can construct them by himself, although their structuration usually coincides with language (except among the deaf and dumb who add a new term – gesture language – to the preceding series). Their common source is imitation, which begins as early as the sensori-motor level, where it already constitutes a kind of representation, though only in actions, and then goes on to deferred or interiorized imitations, whence the preceding symbols.

The second level characteristic of the semeiotic function (a level which, until we know more about it, would seem to be peculiar to the human species) is that of articulated language, of which the two new features as compared with the previous level are, firstly, that it implies social or educational transmission and thus depends upon the whole of society and no longer on individual reactions; and secondly that the verbal *significants* consist of 'signs' and no longer of symbols, the sign being conventional or 'arbitrary' as required by its collective nature.

The first major interdisciplinary questions which such a picture raises then are, firstly, to determine the common mechanisms and the antagonisms in and between various manifestations of the semeiotic function, but going right back to the level of the significant indices and the currently known forms of animal language; and, secondly, to determine their connexion with the development of representation or thought in general, regardless of any possible or more particular relations between articulated language and logic.

The first of these demands collaboration between zoopsychology or ethology, genetic psychology, the psychopathology of aphasia, deaf-mutes, the blind, etc., and linguistics. Ethology has already built up a fairly substantial body of material on the innate releasing mechanisms (IRM) which come into play at the instinctual level and on the releasing mechanisms acquired through learning. Von Frisch's well-known studies on the language of bees have evoked many reactions from psychologists and linguists (Benveniste), while Revesz has undertaken some systematic comparisons of the 'languages' of vertebrates and of man. The general tendency is to regard animal language as being based not on systems of signs but on a 'code of signals' (Benveniste). For one thing, there is neither dialogue nor the free composition of elements; for another, the signals used are essentially imitative or mimetic (though it has not yet been established whether there is already deferred imitation). Such imitative mechanisms thus fall within the sensori-motor pattern, innate or acquired, and do not yet correspond to a conceptualization; whereas in human language not only does every word connote a concept, but the syntactical arrangement of the words itself conveys information.

It is therefore tempting to look for the source of thought itself in sign language, as indeed many psychologists and linguists believe. But although the system of signs has undoubtedly one exceptional advantage on account of its constructive mobility and of the considerable number of meanings which it is capable of conveying, considerations of two kinds regarding the limits of its powers must be remembered.

The first is that although language is a necessary auxiliary to the fulfilment of thought insofar as the latter constitutes interiorized intelligence, it is nonetheless activated by intelligence, which precedes it in its sensori-motor form; this is a problem which we will consider again shortly in connexion with the relations between logic and language. But it must be remembered that, however collective language may be (in its structures, findings, penalties, etc.), it is bound up in its functioning with individual intelligences outside of which its *significants* would have no *signifiés*, and whose sensori-motor pattern itself creates a multitude of meanings (space-time patterns, permanent objects, causality, etc.) which provide the sub-structure of verbal semantics.

Furthermore, the interiorization of the sensori-motor intelligence in image or thought is a matter not just of language but of the entire semeiotic function. In this respect psycho-pathological data are of great interest and much is still awaited from co-operation between linguists, psychologists and neurologists. Without going into the highly complex problem of aphasia, on which much work is still being done but which has so many neurological incidences that the language and thought factors cannot easily be isolated, it is interesting merely to note the case of children deaf-and-dumb, or blind, from birth, but otherwise normal. Among the former there is, of course, some delay in the development of the intellectual operations as compared with children capable of speech, but the fundamental operations of classification, seriation, correspondence, etc., are not missing at all up to a certain level of complexity, which testifies to a pre-speech organization of those actions.[36] Among blind children, on the other hand, the delay appears to be greater because of the lack of a sensori-motor control during the formation of the action patterns, and although language makes good that lack to some extent, it is not enough to replace general co-ordinations and depend upon the latter while their build-up is necessarily retarded.

## 16. *Linguistic structures and logical structures*

The links between linguistics and logic are of unquestioned importance and are still in process of full development, particularly as they impact upon long-standing arguments between psychologists and sociologists.

This, it should first be noted, is no accident. The convergence between the basic ideas of a linguistic doctrine like F. de Saussure's and a sociological theory like Durkheim's is quite remarkable: language is a collective 'institution' transmitted from the outside and imposing itself upon individuals; any innovations made by the latter must accord with common rules established before them, and their initiatives are subject to the approval of the linguistic group, which may reject or accept them, but in the latter case only because of needs related to the overall equilibrium of the system, etc. Now Durkheim drew from his ideas on the social totality the conclusion that the rules of logic are imposed by the group upon the individual, in particular through language, the shaper of intelligences and the holder of structures which are imposed from childhood through education.

Current trends in social and cultural anthropology are moving in the same direction, and we all know how much the structuralism of Lévi-Strauss has been influenced by Saussurian linguistics and by phonology (Troubetskoy and Jakobson), in that the system of meanings seems to him to throw light both on the economic exchanges of tribal societies and on the relations of kinship, the latter comprising a logic that is at one and the same time collective and a source of individual manipulations (hence his opposition to Lévy-Bruhl's pre-logic which Durkheim also contested for similar reasons).

But these trends in linguistic sociology have come up against a completely different tendency. The vast logical positivism movement (developed by the 'Vienna Circle') has attempted, while reducing experimental truths to simple perceived facts, to make allowance for the logico-mathematical arrangement of knowledge, but without seeing in it a source of truth in a strict sense: it conceived of it, in the nominalist tradition, as mere language, while characterizing this linguistic status more precisely. R. Carnap began by proposing that all logic should be reduced to a general syntax, which the natural languages would reflect with various degrees of faithfulness but the exact image of which would be supplied by the formalized language of modern symbolic logic. Tarski, followed by Carnap, then showed the need for a general semantic system or meta-language designed to establish meanings; and finally Morris, though not with everyone's support, proposed the constitution of a 'pragmatic' system, though purely in the sense of the establishment of the rules of such 'languages'.

These concepts have been applauded by a number of linguists and in the *Encyclopedia of Unified Sciences* Bloomfield vigorously applauds the disappearance of the naïve idea that concepts must still be sought beneath the logical or mathematical liaisons: nothing exists except the observable, perceived fact and the system of signs, whether natural (current languages) or scientific, used to describe or connote it.

Yet this dual sociological and linguistic movement (whose unity through convergence is, however, still remarkable, despite the wide gap between the normative realism of Durkheim and the more or less conventional nominalism of the 'logical empiricists') is in fact being contested, and in senses that are again convergent but opposed to the previous ones, by a great deal of research now being conducted by psychologists, linguists and logicians.

On the psychological plane the author for years has been trying (and these studies are in full swing with the co-operation of linguists) to show that the sources of the logico-mathematical structures are to be sought at a deeper level than language, i.e. at the level of the general co-ordination of actions. At the level of sensori-motor intelligence one finds indeed, in the make-up of the patterns of action and in the co-ordination of those patterns, structures of interlocking elements, of order correspondence, etc., which are already of a logical nature and which lie at the start of future thought operations. Moreover, the operations themselves are more closely connected with the interiorization and regulating mechanisms than with the purely verbal influences. It is not until we reach the higher levels that a logic of 'propositions' becomes possible in liaison with the handling of hypotheses enunciated verbally; whereas a whole period of 'concrete' operations, i.e. operations bearing directly upon the object, points to the lasting liaison between those operations and material action.

From the linguistic point of view it then becomes possible to carry out precise experiments on the correlations between the linguistic structure of the verbal expressions used by the child and the latter's operational level; the results of those experiments tend to prove that the language employed is subordinate to the operational structures rather than vice-versa.[37]

As regards that interminable 'dialogue of the deaf' between sociologists and psychologists as to whether 'universal' logic, meaning applicable to all individuals, is superimposed on society or is only a product of it, the two opposing contentions are in fact out of date, in that although logic is concerned with the general co-ordination of action, that co-ordination is as much inter-individual as intra-individual: and indeed, the operations occurring in cognitive exchanges are found upon analysis to be the same as in individual constructions, so that the former are as much a source of the latter as vice versa, the two remaining inseparable by reason of their common biological roots.

On the other hand the linguists, while continuing their structuralist analyses and in particular while attempting to formalize them as precisely as possible in order to express the structural liaisons in a language based on algebraic and sometimes even on physical methods, were far from ending up with a simple logic, but discovered instead a series of structures *sui generis* and peculiar to sign systems as such. This result is of two-fold interest, firstly because it shows how a system of signs differs from a system of intellectual norms of truths, and secondly because it brings up the problem of the relationship between the two. And that relationship certainly exists, for while signs have their own laws, it is also their function, within the active range of the subjects of the language, to express meanings which are of a logical nature in varying degrees. It was in this way that Hjelmslev, the linguist, came to propound the theory of a 'sub-logical' level where connexions are formed between logical and linguistic co-ordinations. It would seem very likely that analysis of that sub-logic would bring us back to questions of co-ordination of action.

It must however be remembered, in particular, that linguistic structuralism, which was essentially static with F. de Saussure, has become dynamic since Z. Harris stressed the 'creative' aspect of language and since N. Chomsky discovered his 'transformational grammar', which makes it possible to derive from a 'fixed kernel', which he regards as innate, an indefinite number of terms in accordance with precise rules of transformation (and in conformity with a 'monoïde' ordinal and associative structure). Now Chomsky attributes his 'innate fixed kernel' to reason itself, which is the complete reverse of the positivist position of the linguists (Bloomfield, etc.). One can, of course, without in any way changing the purely linguistic aspects of Chomsky's doctrine, query his innateness of reason, since the sensori-motor intelligence which precedes language is the end-product of a long structuration in which the hereditary factors (which play a part everywhere) are far from being the only ones involved; and H. Sinclair is currently trying to demonstrate that the constitution of the 'monoïde' could be explained as the co-ordination of the sensori-motor patterns. It is nonetheless true that, in the very sphere of linguistics, we have here a reversal of the subordination of logical structures to language, thus opening up a very broad field of experimental research to interdisciplinary collaboration (psycholinguistics, etc.) in the study of questions which have hitherto mainly been dealt with in a speculative fashion.

Furthermore, those logicians who, venturing beyond the problems of pure formalization, look into the question of the relations between logical structures and the activities of the subject, steer naturally in the direction of self-regulating systems capable of taking account of the self-correction proper to logical mechanisms. Now cybernetics, which can supply such models, is a synthesis of the information or communication theories and of the guiding or regulatory theories. It is thus on this two-fold plane that a more natural relationship than a simple and straightforward assimilation can be established between linguistics and logic. On the one hand language is information, and various relationships are conceivable between the praxeological aspects of the codes and their logical structure. It was along these lines that L. Apostel studied language as a system for the pre-correction of errors. Again, logical operations constitute the extreme case of thought regulation, and there can be many intermediate stages, capable of influencing the language, between the weakest forms of such regulation and the strictest or operational forms. It can thus be seen how interdisciplinary research, in this field also, is both necessary and promising.

## 17. *The higher symbolisms*

The general semeiology advocated by F. de Saussure provides, as we saw in section 15, for systematic comparisons between the sign systems and various symbolisms or signallings inferior in nature to articulated language. But it also presupposes comparisons with what could be called symbolisms to the second power, or of a nature superior to language, that is to say using language but constituting '*signifiants*' whose collective meanings are ideological and situated on a different scale from verbal semantics: such, for example, are the myths, folklore stories, etc., which are conveyed through language but each of which is itself a symbol with a religious or affective meaning conforming to very general semantic laws, as their surprising and frequently intercontinental dissemination shows.

However, the problem is not an easy one to master or even to set. In a nominalistic conception of logic and mathematics, it could be said that any concept or particular structure is still a sign which symbolizes, together with but in addition to the words designating it, the objects to which it applies: thus the notion of a mathematical 'group' would merely be a higher symbol whose meaning would be reduced to the different displacements, physical states, etc., which can be described by it. In the operative sense, on the other hand, the 'group' or any other logical or mathematical concept constitutes a system of actions impacting on the real, which are true actions even though interiorized and which would therefore have nothing symbolic in themselves, the symbolism coming in the arbitrary signs designating the operations but not in the operations as such.

If this latter interpretation is accepted, not all thought is necessarily symbolic, but symbolism reappears in all forms of thought whose value is linked not to its operative structure but to its affective content, conscious or unconscious: in such an interpretation there is nonetheless an immense field of human productions, with the more or less individual 'symbolic thought' studied by the psychoanalysts of different schools, the mythological and folklore symbols, the art symbols and lastly perhaps certain forms of ideologies as they express momentary collective values and not rational structures (each of these manifestations, of course, being capable of 'rationalization' to some degree). It can be seen that at these levels there is a substantial field of comparison open to a general semeiology and that the latter, inspired by linguistic methods, would be no less essentially interdisciplinary.

Freudian psychoanalysis, helped in this instance by Bleuler's work on 'autistic' thought and followed by Jung's dissident school, brought to light the existence of an individual 'symbolic thought' visible in dreams, in childrens' play and in various pathological manifestations. Its criterion is that whereas rational thought seeks adequation with the real, the function of symbolic thought is the direct satisfaction of desires through the subordination of representations to affectivity. Freud began by explaining this unconscious symbolism as camouflage mechanisms due to repression, but later came round to the broader conception of Blueler who, with his 'autism', explained symbolism as a centring on the ego, and he pursued his research in the direction of art symbols. Jung, on the other hand, quickly saw that this symbolism constituted a sort of affective language and, as a result of large-scale comparisons with mythologies, came to demonstrate the fairly universal nature of a great many symbols or 'archetypes' which he considered, without giving proof, as being hereditary, but which are very widespread – which is quite another thing.

The link thus established between the more or less subconscious symbolism which the psychoanalysts find in individuals and the mythological artistic symbolism (one recalls the typical example of the Oedipus myth and 'complex') is evidence that the laws of such a symbolism concern collective as much as psychological realities. It therefore goes without saying that in the field of social and cultural anthropology the direct study of mythical representations provides a contribution of vital importance to this general semeiology at the level above language; and when Lévi-Strauss, for example, conceives of it in Saussurian terms he thereby introduces into this vast and difficult field an indispensable methodology which was only too lacking in the analyses of Jung and Freud.

Nevertheless that is merely the beginning of the work, for obviously laws which are general at a certain scale of civilization must have some applications in societies which are familiar with scientific thought. When K. Marx raised the problem of the opposition between economic and technical infrastructures and ideological superstructures, he brought up in doing so a considerable number of questions regarding the nature and functioning of the various possible types of ideological productions. To show how necessary it is to raise these questions, it is worth recalling that one of the most determined adversaries of the Marxist docrines, V. Pareto, brought into his sociology a distinction which was visibly based on them: for it was Pareto's view that social behaviour patterns are governed by certain needs or affective invariants which he calls the 'residues'; but these – and this is the only point which interests us – are in fact manifested not in naked or direct form but wrapped up in all manner of concepts, doctrines, etc., which Pareto calls 'derivations'. It is thus immediately apparent that these 'derivations' constitute an ideological superstructure, but one of an essentially symbolic nature since it comprises essential and constant affective meanings beneath a variable and secondary conceptual mechanism.

In this chapter, whose purpose is to seek out the common mechanisms and to stress the interdisciplinary problems from a methodological and, particularly, from a prospective point of view, mention must be made, because of its highly significant implications, of the research bearing upon the symbolic meaning of doctrines of intellectual form and affective content, since such research constitutes a striking meeting-point between the possible extensions of a general semeiology bearing upon higher-level symbolic systems and the sociological and even economic analysis of Marxian inspiration. One remarkable example of such meeting-points has been supplied by L. Goldmann in his studies on Jansenism, and our reason for choosing this example is that it forms one of those somewhat rare cases in sociology where through theoretical research the existence of a hitherto unknown fact – in this particular case the discovery of an historical person but one overlooked by history – has been predicated. Goldmann explained Jansenism by the social and economic difficulties of the *noblesse de robe* under Louis xiv: the complete withdrawal from the world preached by the doctrine was thus the symbolic manifestation of an affective and collective situation. But pure Jansenism, as reconstituted through this analysis in terms of social symbolism, was not fully realised in any of the individuals known to history (Arnauld, etc.), and it was therefore necessary to build up the complete hypothetical Jansenist – unknown precisely because completely consistent – who had directed the movement without being seen outside. Having thus 'calculated', so to speak, the existence of such a leader, Goldmann went on to find him in the person of the Abbé Barcos and proceeded to demonstrate his effective and until then unsuspected rôle in history.

One can thus see the number of literary, artistic and metaphysical productions which could emerge from such analyses, the syntactic and semantic aspects of which remain essential even though the most difficult to distinguish, and whose sociological and even economic aspects are obvious.

## 18. *Diachronic and synchronic problems in relation to meanings*

Comte's sociology drew a distinction between static problems ('order') and dynamic ones ('progress'), but the Saussurian linguistic system was probably the first to give a positive status to the relative opposition of synchronic and diachronic considerations in the human sciences. The history of language and the etymology of words do not explain everything, since the meanings of words change, just as the function of biological organs may change, to meet the needs created by the balance of the language as it is at a particular point of time.

Now, systems of meanings as relations between the *signifiant* and the *signifié* occupy a special position in regard to the connexion between synchronic balance and diachronic transformations. As we have seen (paragraph 9), the *maximum* dependence between these two aspects is to be found in the sphere of normative structures, because the evolution of norms – the operational structures of the intelligence, for example – is a process of gradual equilibration: this being so, the nearer the structure under consideration is to its state of final closure (which, it should be added, in no wise excludes the possibility of its being subsequently integrated into new structures) the more closely, of course, does the synchronic balance depend upon this same self-regulating process. We have seen an intermediate situation (section 14) in the case of values, whose dependence upon their history increases the more closely they are linked with structures (normative values) and the less nearly they correspond to the needs of a changing function. As for the *'signifiants'* that operate in systems of meaning, it is obvious that the more conventional or 'arbitrary' they are, the more subordinate to the needs of the moment and the more independent of the previous history they will be. It is therefore in these situations that we find the *minimum* of relationship between present balance and diachrony. This can be seen, for instance, in a system of artificial, technical signs such as mathematical language. Fundamentally, the choice of signs such as $A \times B$, $A \cdot B$ or $AB$ to express multiplication, or of any particular sign for other operations, depends only on the conventions of the time, and not on the history of symbols, which in any case comprises series of transformations that are explicable, but usually linked to the very overall balance of the system at each period under consideration; fidelity to the past may even be a disturbing factor rather than a useful one, if it hinders the reorganization of perspectives, which would on the contrary be facilitated by a new symbolism.

It is true that *'signifiants'* can be divided, as F. de Saussure pointed out (and Peirce earlier, although his method of classification does not seem so logical) into motivated 'symbols' and arbitrary 'signs', and that there are transition series between the two. The very notion of the arbitrary nature of the sign has given rise to discussion, by Jespersen in the past and by Jakobson today. De Saussure, however, appears to have answered these objections before they were raised, by himself distinguishing between the 'relatively arbitrary' and the 'radically arbitrary'. Broadly speaking, it does seem to be true that the word used to designate a concept has not as close a relationship to it (relationship between the phonic subject and the meaning of the idea) as the concept has with its meaning and its content. Even if the verbal signs are sometimes accompanied by symbolism (in the Saussurian sense of a relationship of resemblance or motivation between that which symbolizes and that which is symbolized) and even if, as far as the speaker is aware, there is nothing arbitrary about the word (as Benveniste has pointed out), it seems obvious that the multiplicity of languages bears witness to this conventional nature of the verbal sign. Signs, moreover, are always social (explicit or implicit conventions originating in usage), whereas the symbol may have an individual origin, as in the symbolic games of children, or in dreams.

The problem raised by linguists of the relationship between synchronic and diachronic factors in the sphere of relations between structures and meanings is very broad in scope, and to study it may help us to understand various interdisciplinary questions, such as those of the interpretation – which may be linguistic or, on the other hand, operative and constructive – of logical and mathematical structures. If we accept the nominalist hypothesis, according to which these structures are a mere language used to express experiential data, the relations between their syntax and their semantic should obey the general laws that govern their synchronic and diachronic relations. And at first sight, this indeed appears to be the case: syntactical rules are continuous in time, while meanings vary. The theorems of Euclidian geometry are true today, even though they have changed in meaning, mainly for two reasons: first, they do not seem to us today to be the expression of a unique, necessary form of space, as Kant still thought; we see them as one of several systems of measurement, and this undoubtedly alters their meaning, enriching it, moreover, with all the possible transitions between Euclidian and non-Euclidian structures; the other reason, which is still more general, is that spatial forms do not appear to us today as static figures, but as the results of transformations, so that each form of geometry is subordinated to a basic 'group' of transformations, and that these groups give birth to each other in the same way as sub-groups can be differentiated within a main group. But although these meanings depend, at every point in history, on the synchronic system of knowledge under consideration at that moment, they do not succeed each other at random, as if they were the result of accidents or exogenous factors; proceeding by reflective abstraction from previous states of construction, new inventions which alter meanings are in line with a progressive equilibration in which the synchronic balance is at once the result and the starting-point of new constructive processes. In this respect, therefore, the situation is considerably different from that of the 'natural' languages, in which synchronic balance is a question of re-equilibrations that are governed by a great many external and internal factors.

This problem of the relationship between synchronic balance and diachronic evolution gives rise to another closely-allied problem – that of the nature of the innovations which change human behaviour in the course of history and necessitate re-equilibrations. Here we may identify three possible types of innovation, which play a very different rôle in the relations of approximate continuity or discontinuity between present equilibrium and previous equilibration processes. The first of these types of innovation is that of 'discoveries', which bring to light what was already in existence, independently of the subject, but which was not known or perceived before (for instance, the discovery of America). Obviously, in such a case, the necessary re-equilibrations are not determined solely by the previous states of the system. Secondly, we speak of 'inventions', when new combinations emerge as a result of the actions of the human subject (without going back to what some biologists have called organic 'inventions' in relation to highly differentiated organs that are specially adapted to a new situation). It is the property of an invention that, however well the components that are combined may have been known (so that the innovation is only a matter of making the actual combination for the first time), yet the invention could have been a different one; to invent a new symbolism, for instance, does not imply that others could not have been invented instead. It is obvious that in such cases also present re-equilibrations and past history are relatively independent. There is, however, a third type of innovation in human behaviour, which can have considerable social significance; it is sometimes called 'invention' and sometimes 'discovery' in relation to logico-mathematical structures or the structures of intelligence in general. Mathematical 'invention', however, is not a 'discovery' (unless one is a Platonist), since it is a new combination; the imaginary number $\sqrt{-1}$, for example, is the result of a combination, made by Cardan, of the negative number and the extraction of the root. Nor is it simply an invention, since once it is accomplished one must admit that it could not have been different, and that it therefore arose of necessity from within its own laws. It is in this third case (many examples of which are to be found in the sphere of mental development, in the spontaneous formation of logical structures) that synchronic re-equilibration depends closely upon previous evolution, because diachronic constructions, even at that stage, were based on progressive equilibration, and because the present balance is the (provisional) termination of such a process..

V. CONCLUSION: THE SUBJECT OF KNOWLEDGE AND THE HUMAN SCIENCES

The social and human sciences have their own series of epistemological problems. But there are two quite distinct types of question to be considered in this connexion: questions concerning the research worker as such, or, in other words, those that are proper to the epistemology of his branch of study as a particular form of scientific knowledge; and those that concern the subject of study himself, who, since he is a human being, is a source of knowledge and indeed the starting-point of all the knowledge – whether artless, technical, scientific, etc. – available to the various societies, which is the origin of the human sciences. By grouping interdisciplinary problems around realities – structures or rules, values and meanings – that are common to them all, we have referred to the three great manifestations of the activity of this natural subject; it remains in conclusion for us to see how the human sciences regard this subject as a subject, for this is perhaps one of the most promising points of convergence to be kept in mind for the future, although it has not yet been sufficiently analysed.

19. *The development of knowledge and the epistemology of the human subject*

All the social and human sciences are more or less closely concerned, in their diachronic aspects, with the development of knowledge. The economic history of human societies would not be complete without a history of techniques, and the latter is of basic importance in relation to the growth of the sciences. Prehistorical anthropology is an extension of these studies, and brings in all the problems of the transition from behaviour involving the use of tools (which has been studied closely among the Anthropoids) to techniques in the proper sense. Social and cultural anthropology opens up extremely important questions concerning the formation of group pre-logic or logic, as related to social and family organization, economic life, myths and language. And this problem of logic in tribal civilizations has by no means been solved; indeed, it requires not only detailed psychological experimentation, which has not yet been developed in this comparative form, but also careful comparison, in each society, between practical or technical intelligence and discursive or merely verbal thought. Linguistics provides us with basic material concerning the oral or written expression of cognitive structures such as numeration systems, classifications, systems of relations and so on.

The two main branches of science, in connexion with the formation of the tools of cognition – the sociology of knowledge and genetic psychology – are complementary. The socio-genesis of knowledge shows us both the progressive, co-operative construction of movements of ideas as they are transmitted and developed, from one generation to another, and the effects of the numerous obstacles that slow down or divert the progress of ideas. The historical sociology of knowledge, for instance, which is bound to depend increasingly on the history of ideas, sciences and techniques, should be able to throw light on phenomena as momentous as the Greek miracle or the decay of Greek knowledge in the time of Alexander, and it will at once be seen that this last problem, for which the human sciences should provide some solution, cannot be solved except by comparing economic and social factors with the inner evolution of concepts and principles whose initial imperatives might furnish reasons for their subsequent sterility.

Genetic psychology and comparative psychology (including ethology) are far from dealing with such central facts, but their great advantage is that they are concerned with series that are not so incomplete and, most important, can be reproduced at will. An example of this is the construction of whole or 'natural' numbers. All the data collected by the foregoing branches of knowledge show that the elaboration of such numbers is common in the different civilizations, and also that the levels reached differ widely, but none of these facts show us the construction itself; we know only its results. On the other hand, although a young child is surrounded by adults who teach him to count, and although the form of expression he uses includes a system of numeration, yet one can easily, by means of carefully-planned experiments, go back to stages where the term 'numbers' cannot yet be used because numerical sets are not conserved (5 items are not 5 if their arrangement in space is changed, and so on), and by starting at such stages it is possible to observe the mechanism by which number is constituted through purely logical operations, yet by making a fresh synthesis of the operations of inclusion and arrangement in order. Such information, therefore, throws light on ethnographic and historical data, which would be superfluous if we could go back to the mental activity of prehistoric man – but that, unhappily, is impossible in a sphere such as the origin of number. On the other hand, information of this kind gives rise to fresh problems of logic, and not only has this genetic construction been formalized (J. B. Grize and G. Granger), but it has also been shown that, implicitly but necessarily, its essential aspects were found in all the models elaborated by logicians concerning the transition from classes or relations to numbers. Thirdly, it is instructive to compare such facts with zoopsychological data as to the way in which animals learn about numbers (experiments carried out by W. Köhler and others).

Another instructive example is that of notions of space, for which we have ample ethnographic and historical data, but again insufficient information about the way in which they were arrived at. But in this sphere we find a somewhat paradoxical situation as regards relations between history and theory. For the history of geometry shows that the Greeks began by systematizing the properties of Euclidean space in a remarkable way. They also had certain intuitions about projective space, but did not succeed in establishing an analogy or in evolving any really topological theory. Projective geometry did not emerge as an independent branch of science until the seventeenth century, and topology finally came into its own in the nineteenth century – at the time when non-Euclidian geometries were being discovered. But from the standpoint of theoretical construction, topology is the starting-point of the geometrical edifice, and from it proceed projective geometry on the one hand and general metrics on the other (whence the differentiation between Euclidian and non-Euclidian). Now genetic psychology and studies of perception show that natural development is actually nearer to theory than to history, the latter having inverted the genetic order by starting with the results and only subsequently going back to the sources (a common proceeding, which of itself demonstrates the value of comparisons between psychological genesis and historical evolution). For on the one hand the study of the formation of space structures in children shows that topological structures precede the two others and are the pre-requisite of their formation, whilst later on projective and Euclidian structures emerge concurrently. On the other hand, Luneburg thought he could prove that elementary perceptive space was Riemannian and not Euclidian (perception of parallels, etc.), which is perhaps an exaggeration, but at least appears to show that there is an undifferentiated situation from which Euclidian structures are organized only secondarily.

Many other examples could be given concerning the notions of time, speed, causality and so on, and physicists have even been known to use the findings of psychogenesis as to the initial independence of ordinal ideas of speed as related to duration. Thus the facts that have been ascertained, taken together, show that interdisciplinary collaboration is possible in the sphere of the epistemology of the human subject in general, and that this epistemology of natural thought links up with the great problems of the epistemology of scientific knowledge. This is a special case of the study of structures (under II), but it has a very wide significance.

## 20. *Re-combination through 'hybridization'*

The foregoing considerations show that the human sciences, in so far as they necessarily include in their field of study the subject of knowledge – the source of the logical and mathematical structures on which indeed they depend – do not merely maintain a set of interdisciplinary relations between one another, the need for which we attempted to demonstrate in Parts I–IV, but are part of an extensive circuit or network that really covers all the sciences (this was clear in any case owing to their relations with biology; cf. section 2). It was essential to recall this so as to be able to shape our conclusions in such a way that they might succeed in revealing the true significance of interdisciplinary relations.

For their significance far exceeds that of a mere tool for facilitating work, which is all they would amount to if used solely in a common exploration of the boundaries of knowledge. This way of viewing collaboration between specialists in different branches of knowledge would be the only possible one if we admitted a thesis to which far too many research workers still unwittingly cling – that the frontiers of each branch of science are fixed once and for all, and that they will inevitably remain so in the future. But the main object of a work such as this, a work that deals with trends and not with results, with the perspectives and the prospective study of the human sciences and not merely with their present state, is rather to make clear that in fact the object of any innovatory trend is to push back the frontiers horizontally and to challenge them transversally. The true object of interdisciplinary research, therefore, is to reshape or reorganize the fields of knowledge by means of exchanges which are in fact constructive recombinations.

Indeed, one of the most striking features of the scientific movements of recent years is the increased number of new branches of knowledge born precisely from the union of neighbouring fields of study, but in fact adopting new goals that impact upon the parent sciences and enrich them. We might speak of a sort of 'hybridization' between two fields of study that were originally heterogeneous, but the metaphor is meaningless unless the term 'hybrid' is understood not in the meaning it had in classical biology fifty years ago, when hybrids were thought of as infertile, or at least impure, but as the 'genetic recombinations' of contemporary biology, which prove more balanced and better adapted than pure genotypes, and which are gradually replacing mutations in our conceptions of the mechanism of evolution. There are many fruitful hybridizations in the natural sciences, from topological algebra to biophysics, biochemistry and the young science of quantum biophysics. A movement of much smaller scope but comparable in spirit has produced several new branches of study in the sciences of man and we may by way of conclusion describe these hybridizations, trying to bring out their productive significance for the parent sciences from which they sprang.

Those branches of knowledge which have come into being simply through the refinement of mathematical or statistical methods and through being more closely synthesized with experimentation should not be classified amongst these new branches of knowledge born of re-combinations. Econometry, for instance, may in one sense enrich mathematics, but solely because of the problems it produces for mathematics to solve. The games theory was known to Emile Borel (1921–1927) quite apart from its applications to economics, and the mathematician Von Neumann's general theorem *(minimum maximorum)* dates from 1928, whereas his collaboration with the economist Morgenstern dates from 1937. Nevertheless, as we have seen, the study of economic behaviour has established valuable links with psychology and other sciences, and there is no need to mention the numerous other applications of the games theory.

On the other hand, a genuine 'hybridization', with fruitful re-combinations, is that of psycholinguistics, for it enriches both psychology – obviously – and linguistics itself, inasmuch as only this new branch of science leads to systematic studies of the individual's use of language, which, on the contrary, is institutionalized. Doubtless much, too, may be expected from 'sociolinguistics', in which Greenberg and others have undertaken studies combining linguistics and sociology.

Social psychology is as useful to sociology as to psychology, on which it confers a new dimension; and while social psychologists sometimes display that kind of imperialism that is the mark of a science in its youth, it is also a sign of independence and an augury of syntheses to come.

Ethology, or zoopsychology, is today undertaken by professional zoologists as much as – indeed, more than – by psychologists, and it unquestionably enriches biology (especially with regard to the theory of selection, by showing that the animal chooses and fashions his environment as much as it is conditioned by the latter), while at the same time it makes a unique contribution to psychology, in particular in the analysis of the cognitive functions (instinct, learning and intelligence).

The author must be forgiven for laying equal stress on the experiment undertaken in genetic epistemology in the last ten years or so, or the study of the formation and building up of knowledge. In the study of the development of logical, mathematical, kinematical and other structures, the international centre set up for this purpose in Geneva has always encouraged psychologists to collaborate with logicians, mathematicians, cyberneticians, physicists and so on. Now, genetic epistemology is on the one hand a new branch of science, which results from the hybridization of epistemology (especially in its 'historico-critical' methods) and genetic psychology. And it serves both at once, for, as the logician S. Papert has said, in order to understand man we must know something of epistemology, and in order to understand epistemology we must have a knowledge of man.

In a sense, therefore, the situation of these new and essentially interdisciplinary branches of science confirms what was said (in section 1) about situations in which the link between a 'higher' (in the sense of 'more complex') and a 'lower' field results neither in a reduction of the first to the second nor in greater heterogeneity of the first, but in mutual assimilation such that the second explains the first, but does so by enriching itself with properties not previously perceived, which afford the necessary link. In the case of the human sciences, in which there can be no question of growing complexity or of declining generality, because all aspects are to be found everywhere, and because delimitation of the different fields is a process of abstraction rather than a question of hierarchy, mutual assimilation is still more necessary and there is no danger of vitiating the specificity of phenomena. The difficulties, however, are considerable. But, apart from the difference between various forms of university training, which is undoubtedly the main obstacle to be overcome, the common logico-mathematical techniques that are gradually coming into general use are at once the best indication of the convergence that is called for and the best means of effecting a junction.

NOTES

1. See N. CHOMSKY, *Cartesian Linguistics*, London, 1966.
2. It is worth mentioning, though, that F. de Saussure took inspiration from economic doctrines of equilibrium when founding his synchronic structuralism. But he might just as easily have based his distinctions on that between organ and function in biology.
3. For instance, Schmalhausen.
4. In this connexion cf. J. F. BERGIER and L. SOLARI, *Pour une méthodologie des sciences économiques*, Geneva, Librairie de l'Université, 1965, p. 15, where J. F. Bergier refers to 'a verification of the mechanisms of price formation insofar as these are timeless and imperative', an opinion on which Chapter IV shows that economists are not always in agreement.
5. On the contrary, it is clear that different degrees and types of balancing or controls giving a direction must be distinguished. Soviet authors, while emphasizing that the mechanisms of retroaction are an indispensable attribute of the higher degrees of organization of structures, maintain that 'plan regulators' are necessarily accompanied by 'regulators of statistical structure', which are not identical with them (see Y. A. LEVADA, 'Knowledge and Direction in Social Processes', *Voprosy filosofii* 5, 1956).

    As for the problems of typology in general, they are studied closely in economics and linguistics, less effectively in psychology and sociology. But it is doubtful whether they could lead to interdisciplinary research at the present time (except in economics and sociology), for the 'types' differ considerably from one field to another.
6. For this comparison see J. PIAGET, *Le structuralisme*, Paris, P.U.F., 1968, translation London, 1971.
7. If the human subject or the social group were more than centres of functioning, if they constituted a 'structure of all the structures' (which is impossible both because of the known categorical antinomies and because of the theorems on the limits of formalization), they would merge with the 'transcendental subject' of *a priori* idealism.
8. This does not mean, as just stated, that consciousness is *cause*, since it remains parallel to its physiological concomitants; but it involves systems of meanings mutually connected by implications, in isomorphism with the sequences of neurological causality.
9. B. PEKLOV, 'Ueber Norminferenzen', *Logique et Analyse* 28, 1964, pp. 203–211.
10. O. WEINBERGER, 'Einige Betrachtungen über die Rechtnorm vom Standpunkt des Logik und der Semantik', *Logique et Analyse* 28, 1964, pp. 212–232.
11. It should be noted in particular that these trends of relational structuralism show considerable similarity with those of research in epistemology and methodology in the works of a certain number of Soviet authors (V. I. Kremyanski, Y. A. Levada, G. P. Chtchedrovitski, V. N. Sadovski, V. A. Lektorski, E. G. Youdine, etc.).
12. True, one may wonder what the term 'operation' signifies in a social system. But if we define an operation as an action which is capable of interiorisation, reversible and related to other operations within an overall structure, it is clear that operations occur in all inter-individual actions which are not based solely on relations of force or authority and in all collective actions where norms apply, in short wherever a trace of rationality can be found in a social system (which is by no means exceptional).
13. When we say 'translated in the consciousness' this means that the causality involved should not be sought within the consciousness but in the underlying structures of which the subject's consciousness knows only the results, which he translates into terms of implications (see the end of section 3).
14. A 'normative fact' is the establishment by the sociologist (in sociology of law, etc.) of the fact that the subject recognizes a norm as binding upon him; by establishing

this fact the observer merely notes it without himself adopting any position normatively, i.e. without evaluating the norm of the subject under study.

15. The rôle of language in colour perception has been studied but the effect is arguable. Bruner and Postman's celebrated experiments on estimations of the diameter of a dollar coin or of any disc, varying with the subject's economic level, have not been generally confirmed and are moreover open to other interpretations (centration effects) in those cases where they may possibly have been verified.

16. Exception should be made for N. Chomsky who believes that grammars have an 'innate fixed kernel'; but one is entitled to wonder from the psychological point of view whether the rational fixed kernel does not result from the balancing of the sensori-motor mechanisms whose constitution precedes language and is only partially programmed by heredity.

17. Cf. the problem of 'rôle conflicts' (N. Gross, etc.).

18. Cf. *inter alia* 'La théorie de l'argumentation. Perspectives et applications', *Logique et Analyse*, nos. 21 to 24, 1963.

19. We should mention the important and still lively movement created by Petrazycki, to which we shall refer in section 12.

20. This problem coincides with one of the aspects of the question of relations between logic and history as they are formulated in Marxist literature: the relation of historical continuity in the formation of a system with structural dependence within the system under consideration (this as a reaction against the 'unhistorical' approach still so frequent in certain disciplines).

21. Cf. *inter alia* the collective work edited by T. PARSONS and E. SHILS, *Toward a Theory of Action*, London, in which a number of ethnologists, sociologists and psychologists collaborated. Cf. also the comparative essay by Clyde Kluckhohn defining the rôle of the notion of value in various disciplines (as well as the many definitions proposed by the authors).

22. In the present-day mathematical sense function is defined as an 'application' or an oriented couple, which psychologically makes its origin go back to the general patterns of action. Cf. *Epistémologie et psychologie de la fonction*, Etudes d'Epistémologie génétique, vol. XXIII.

23. Mention should also be made of the conception of 'systems' of a group of researchers from the Case Institute of Technology in Ohio (M. Mezarovitch, R. Akkof, D. Fleming, etc.), the theory of systems developed by L. Zade (a much wider class essentially of a technical nature), the conception of O. Lange, and the numerous works of theoretical research in relation with 'man-machine' systems (e.g. within the framework of the System Development Corporation of California).

24. This does not mean that the translation of processes into cybernetic language automatically allows the mathematization which might be hoped for from that language; however, the fact that questions are formulated in qualitative terms of interactions may in itself constitute an advance because it means a liberation from one-way forms of causality.

25. Pathology is not merely a matter of affective aspects. Let us make clear that while affectivity as energetic functioning can naturally be the cause of accelerations or retardations in the formation of structures (since energy affects speed among other things), this does not mean that it intervenes causally in the structure as such, or vice versa.

26. Cf. primary and secondary utility as distinguished in section 3.

27. See J. PIAGET, *Etudes sociologiques*, Droz, 1965, pp. 100–142.

28. It is not within the scope of this volume to discuss the general problem of measurement. The human sciences have no units comparable to those available in physics; in the sphere of values the difficulty is overcome by the establishment of various scales (ordinal, super-ordinal, etc.), examples of which may be found in *Variations in Value Orientations* by F. R. KLUCKHOHN and F. F. STRODTBECK; their significance may be ascertained by reference to the well-known works of Stevens who, in psychology, has endeavoured to construct a kind of subjective psycho-physics.

29. Avant-garde schools, such as the Polish school, being of course duly excepted.

30. Without wishing to refer here to the mathematical aspects of feedbacks, we may recall that in the case of this simple model the transfer function is in the form

$$F(p) = \frac{v}{s} \text{ where } p = \alpha + iW \text{ and for the 'free variations' of the system } F(p) = 1,$$

hence $W = 0$ and $\alpha = \frac{s}{v}$ in the absence of sinusoidal fluctuations. The latter would appear if delayed reactions between variables were introduced.

31. Supposing that $G(t)$ represents State demand (negative in the case of subsidy), one would obtain, for example, $G(t) = -g \cdot \frac{dY(t)}{dt}$ or $g > 0$, which would constitute a new feedback allowing the rate of growth $f$ to be increased in the form $p' = \frac{s}{v-g}$

32. Let us note further that H. A. Simon ('On the Application of Servomechanism in the Study of Production Control', *Econometrica* 20, 2, 1952, pp. 247–268) has tried to formulate, in situations of a dynamic kind, decision criteria enjoying certain properties of stability. He thus arrived at a loop system making it possible to determine qualitatively a criterion whose intuitive meaning is immediate: the rate of production must be increased or diminished proportionally to the deficit or surplus of effective stocks as compared with optimum stocks and proportionally to the variations of that deficit or surplus.

33. Cf. *inter alia* H. A. Simon's well-known formalization of Festinger's experiments on communication in small social groups.

34. *Logique et connaissance scientifique* (Encyclopédie de la Pléiade), pp. 879–880.

35. It should even be remembered that biologists speak of the transmission of information as early as the genome level, the *significant* then depending on the order of the sequences in the DNA code (Watson and Crick).

36. And collectively as well as individually pre-speech, for among themselves the young deaf-mutes build up a language of gestures.

37. See H. SINCLAIR, *Acquisition du langage et développement de la pensée*, Dunod, 1967.

# Index

# hARpER ⚜ ΤΟRChBOOKS

† The New American Nation Series, edited by Henry Steele Commager and Richard B. Morris.
‡ American Perspectives series, edited by Bernard Wishy and William E. Leuchtenburg.
a History of Europe series, edited by J. H. Plumb.
§ The Library of Religion and Culture, edited by Benjamin Nelson.
Σ Researches in the Social, Cultural, and Behavioral Sciences, edited by Benjamin Nelson.
Ψ Harper Modern Science Series, edited by James A. Newman.
° Not for sale in Canada.
+ Documentary History of the United States series, edited by Richard B. Morris.
# Documentary History of Western Civilization series, edited by Eugene C. Black and Leonard W. Levy.
∧ The Economic History of the United States series, edited by Henry David et al.
¶ European Perspectives series, edited by Eugene C. Black.
** Contemporary Essays series, edited by Leonard W. Levy.
* The Stratum Series, edited by John Hale.

PERRY MILLER: Errand Into the Wilderness
TB/1139
PERRY MILLER & T. H. JOHNSON, Eds.: The Puritans: *A Sourcebook of Their Writings*
Vol. I TB/1093; Vol. II TB/1094
EDMUND S. MORGAN: The Puritan Family: *Religion and Domestic Relations in Seventeenth Century New England* TB/1227
RICHARD B. MORRIS: Government and Labor in Early America TB/1244
WALLACE NOTESTEIN: The English People on the Eve of Colonization: 1603-1630. † *Illus.*
TB/3006
FRANCIS PARKMAN: The Seven Years War: *A Narrative Taken from Montcalm and Wolfe, The Conspiracy of Pontiac, and A Half-Century of Conflict. Edited by John H. McCallum* TB/3083
LOUIS B. WRIGHT: The Cultural Life of the American Colonies: 1607-1763. † *Illus.*
TB/3005
YVES F. ZOLTVANY, Ed.: The French Tradition in America + HR/1425

## American Studies: The Revolution to 1860

JOHN R. ALDEN: The American Revolution: 1775-1783. † *Illus.* TB/3011
MAX BELOFF, Ed.: The Debate on the American Revolution, 1761-1783: *A Sourcebook*
TB/1225
RAY A. BILLINGTON: The Far Western Frontier: 1830-1860. † *Illus.* TB/3012
STUART BRUCHEY: The Roots of American Economic Growth, 1607-1861: *An Essay in Social Causation. New Introduction by the Author.*
TB/1350
WHITNEY R. CROSS: The Burned-Over District: *The Social and Intellectual History of Enthusiastic Religion in Western New York, 1800-1850* TB/1242
NOBLE E. CUNNINGHAM, JR., Ed.: The Early Republic, 1789-1828 + HR/1394
GEORGE DANGERFIELD: The Awakening of American Nationalism, 1815-1828. † *Illus.*
TB/3061
CLEMENT EATON: The Freedom-of-Thought Struggle in the Old South. *Revised and Enlarged. Illus.* TB/1150
CLEMENT EATON: The Growth of Southern Civilization, 1790-1860. † *Illus.* TB/3040
ROBERT H. FERRELL, Ed.: Foundations of American Diplomacy, 1775-1872 + HR/1393
LOUIS FILLER: The Crusade against Slavery: 1830-1860. † *Illus.* TB/3029
DAVID H. FISCHER: The Revolution of American Conservatism: *The Federalist Party in the Era of Jeffersonian Democracy* TB/1449
WILLIAM W. FREEHLING, Ed.: The Nullification Era: *A Documentary Record* ‡ TB/3079
WILLIM W. FREEHLING: Prelude to Civil War: *The Nullification Controversy in South Carolina, 1816-1836* TB/1359
PAUL W. GATES: The Farmer's Age: *Agriculture, 1815-1860* Δ TB/1398
FELIX GILBERT: The Beginnings of American Foreign Policy: *To the Farewell Address*
TB/1200
ALEXANDER HAMILTON: The Reports of Alexander Hamilton. ‡ *Edited by Jacob E. Cooke*
TB/3060
THOMAS JEFFERSON: Notes on the State of Virginia. ‡ *Edited by Thomas P. Abernethy*
TB/3052
FORREST MCDONALD, Ed.: Confederation and Constitution, 1781-1789 + HR/1396

BERNARD MAYO: Myths and Men: *Patrick Henry, George Washington, Thomas Jefferson*
TB/1108
JOHN C. MILLER: Alexander Hamilton and the Growth of the New Nation TB/3057
JOHN C. MILLER: The Federalist Era: 1789-1801. † *Illus.* TB/3027
RICHARD B. MORRIS, Ed.: Alexander Hamilton and the Founding of the Nation. *New Introduction by the Editor* TB/1448
RICHARD B. MORRIS: The American Revolution Reconsidered TB/1363
CURTIS P. NETTELS: The Emergence of a National Economy, 1775-1815 Δ TB/1438
DOUGLASS C. NORTH & ROBERT PAUL THOMAS, Eds.: *The Growth of the American Economy to 1860* + HR/1352
R. B. NYE: The Cultural Life of the New Nation: 1776-1830. † *Illus.* TB/3026
GILBERT OSOFSKY, Ed.: Puttin' On Ole Massa: *The Slave Narratives of Henry Bibb, William Wells Brown, and Solomon Northup* †
TB/1432
JAMES PARTON: The Presidency of Andrew Jackson. *From Volume III of the* Life *of Andrew Jackson. Ed. with Intro. by Robert V. Remini* TB/3080
FRANCIS S. PHILBRICK: The Rise of the West, 1754-1830. † *Illus.* TB/3067
MARSHALL SMELSER: The Democratic Republic, 1801-1815 † TB/1406
TIMOTHY L. SMITH: Revivalism and Social Reform: *American Protestantism on the Eve of the Civil War* TB/1229
JACK M. SOSIN, Ed.: The Opening of the West + HR/1424
GEORGE ROGERS TAYLOR: The Transportation Revolution, 1815-1860 Δ TB/1347
A. F. TYLER: Freedom's Ferment: *Phases of American Social History from the Revolution to the Outbreak of the Civil War. Illus.*
TB/1074
GLYNDON G. VAN DEUSEN: The Jacksonian Era: 1828-1848. † *Illus.* TB/3028
LOUIS B. WRIGHT: Culture on the Moving Frontier TB/1053

## American Studies: The Civil War to 1900

W. R. BROCK: An American Crisis: *Congress and Reconstruction, 1865-67* ° TB/1283
T. C. COCHRAN & WILLIAM MILLER: The Age of Enterprise: *A Social History of Industrial America* TB/1054
W. A. DUNNING: Reconstruction, Political and Economic: 1865-1877 TB/1073
HAROLD U. FAULKNER: Politics, Reform and Expansion: 1890-1900. † *Illus.* TB/3020
GEORGE M. FREDRICKSON: The Inner Civil War: *Northern Intellectuals and the Crisis of the Union* TB/1358
JOHN A. GARRATY: The New Commonwealth, 1877-1890 † TB/1410
JOHN A. GARRATY, Ed.: The Transformation of American Society, 1870-1890 + HR/1395
WILLIAM R. HUTCHISON, Ed.: American Protestant Thought: *The Liberal Era* ‡ TB/1385
HELEN HUNT JACKSON: A Century of Dishonor: *The Early Crusade for Indian Reform.* † *Edited by Andrew F. Rolle* TB/3063
ALBERT D. KIRWAN: Revolt of the Rednecks: *Mississippi Politics, 1876-1925* TB/1199
WILLIAM G. MCLOUGHLIN, Ed.: The American Evangelicals, 1800-1900: An Anthology ‡
TB/1382
ARTHUR MANN: Yankee Reforms in the Urban Age: *Social Reform in Boston, 1800-1900*
TB/1247

ARNOLD M. PAUL: Conservative Crisis and the Rule of Law: *Attitudes of Bar and Bench, 1887-1895. New Introduction by Author*
TB/1415

JAMES S. PIKE: The Prostrate State: *South Carolina under Negro Government. ‡ Intro. by Robert F. Durden*
TB/3085

WHITELAW REID: After the War: *A Tour of the Southern States, 1865-1866. ‡ Edited by C. Vann Woodward*
TB/3066

FRED A. SHANNON: The Farmer's Last Frontier: *...Agriculture, 1860-1897*
TB/1348

VERNON LANE WHARTON: The Negro in Mississippi, 1865-1890
TB/1178

## American Studies: The Twentieth Century

RICHARD M. ABRAMS, Ed.: The Issues of the Populist and Progressive Eras, 1892-1912 +
HR/1428

RAY STANNARD BAKER: Following the Color Line: *American Negro Citizenship in Progressive Era. ‡ Edited by Dewey W. Grantham, Jr. Illus.*
TB/3053

RANDOLPH S. BOURNE: War and the Intellectuals: *Collected Essays, 1915-1919. ‡ Edited by Carl Resek*
TB/3043

A. RUSSELL BUCHANAN: The United States and World War II. † *Illus.*
Vol. I TB/3044; Vol. II TB/3045

THOMAS C. COCHRAN: The American Business System: *A Historical Perspective, 1900-1955*
TB/1080

FOSTER RHEA DULLES: America's Rise to World Power: 1898-1954. † *Illus.*
TB/3021

JEAN-BAPTISTE DUROSELLE: From Wilson to Roosevelt: *Foreign Policy of the United States, 1913-1945. Trans. by Nancy Lyman Roelker*
TB/1370

HAROLD U. FAULKNER: The Decline of Laissez Faire, 1897-1917
TB/1397

JOHN D. HICKS: Republican Ascendancy: 1921-1933. † *Illus.*
TB/3041

ROBERT HUNTER: Poverty: *Social Conscience in the Progressive Era. ‡ Edited by Peter d'A. Jones*
TB/3065

WILLIAM E. LEUCHTENBURG: Franklin D. Roosevelt and the New Deal: 1932-1940. † *Illus.*
TB/3025

WILLIAM E. LEUCHTENBURG, Ed.: The New Deal: *A Documentary History* +
HR/1354

ARTHUR S. LINK: Woodrow Wilson and the Progressive Era: 1910-1917. † *Illus.* TB/3023

BROADUS MITCHELL: Depression Decade: *From New Era through New Deal, 1929-1941* ∧
TB/1439

GEORGE E. MOWRY: The Era of Theodore Roosevelt and the Birth of Modern America: 1900-1912. † *Illus.*
TB/3022

WILLIAM PRESTON, JR.: Aliens and Dissenters: *Federal Suppression of Radicals, 1903-1933*
TB/1287

WALTER RAUSCHENBUSCH: Christianity and the Social Crisis. ‡ *Edited by Robert D. Cross*
TB/3059

GEORGE SOULE: Prosperity Decade: *From War to Depression, 1917-1929* ∧
TB/1349

GEORGE B. TINDALL, Ed.: A Populist Reader: *Selections from the Works of American Populist Leaders*
TB/3069

TWELVE SOUTHERNERS: I'll Take My Stand: *The South and the Agrarian Tradition. Intro. by Louis D. Rubin, Jr.; Biographical Essays by Virginia Rock*
TB/1072

## Art, Art History, Aesthetics

CREIGHTON GILBERT, Ed.: Renaissance Art ** *Illus.*
TB/1465

EMILE MALE: The Gothic Image: *Religious Art in France of the Thirteenth Century.* § *190* illus.
TB/344

MILLARD MEISS: Painting in Florence and Siena After the Black Death: *The Arts, Religion and Society in the Mid-Fourteenth Century. 169 illus.*
TB/1148

ERWIN PANOFSKY: Renaissance and Renascences in Western Art. *Illus.*
TB/1447

ERWIN PANOFSKY: Studies in Iconology: *Humanistic Themes in the Art of the Renaissance. 180 illus.*
TB/1077

JEAN SEZNEC: The Survival of the Pagan Gods: *The Mythological Tradition and Its Place in Renaissance Humanism and Art. 108 illus.*
TB/2004

OTTO VON SIMSON: The Gothic Cathedral: *Origins of Gothic Architecture and the Medieval Concept of Order. 58 illus.*
TB/2018

HEINRICH ZIMMER: Myths and Symbols in Indian Art and Civilization. *70 illus.* TB/2005

## Asian Studies

WOLFGANG FRANKE: China and the West: *The Cultural Encounter, 13th to 20th Centuries. Trans. by R. A. Wilson*
TB/1326

L. CARRINGTON GOODRICH: A Short History of the Chinese People. *Illus.*
TB/3015

DAN N. JACOBS, Ed.: The New Communist Manifesto and Related Documents. *3rd revised edn.*
TB/1078

DAN N. JACOBS & HANS H. BAERWALD, Eds.: Chinese Communism: *Selected Documents*
TB/3031

BENJAMIN I. SCHWARTZ: Chinese Communism and the Rise of Mao
TB/1308

BENJAMIN I. SCHWARTZ: In Search of Wealth and Power: *Yen Fu and the West* TB/1422

## Economics & Economic History

C. E. BLACK: The Dynamics of Modernization: *A Study in Comparative History* TB/1321

STUART BRUCHEY: The Roots of American Economic Growth, 1607-1861: *An Essay in Social Causation. New Introduction by the Author.*
TB/1350

GILBERT BURCK & EDITORS OF *Fortune:* The Computer Age: *And its Potential for Management*
TB/1179

JOHN ELLIOTT CAIRNES: The Slave Power. ‡ *Edited with Introduction by Harold D. Woodman*
TB/1433

SHEPARD B. CLOUGH, THOMAS MOODIE & CAROL MOODIE, Eds.: Economic History of Europe: *Twentieth Century* #
HR/1388

THOMAS C. COCHRAN: The American Business System: *A Historical Perspective, 1900-1955*
TB/1180

ROBERT A. DAHL & CHARLES E. LINDBLOM: Politics, Economics, and Welfare: *Planning and Politico-Economic Systems Resolved into Basic Social Processes*
TB/3037

PETER F. DRUCKER: The New Society: *The Anatomy of Industrial Order* TB/1082

HAROLD U. FAULKNER: The Decline of Laissez Faire, 1897-1917 ∧
TB/1397

PAUL W. GATES: The Farmer's Age: *Agriculture, 1815-1860* ∧
TB/1398

WILLIAM GREENLEAF, Ed.: American Economic Development Since 1860 +
HR/1353

J. L. & BARBARA HAMMOND: The Rise of Modern Industry. || *Introduction by R. M. Hartwell*
TB/1417

3

ROBERT L. HEILBRONER: The Future as History: *The Historic Currents of Our Time and the Direction in Which They Are Taking America* TB/1386

ROBERT L. HEILBRONER: The Great Ascent: *The Struggle for Economic Development in Our Time* TB/3030

FRANK H. KNIGHT: The Economic Organization TB/1214

DAVID S. LANDES: Bankers and Pashas: *International Finance and Economic Imperialism in Egypt. New Preface by the Author* TB/1412

ROBERT LATOUCHE: The Birth of Western Economy: *Economic Aspects of the Dark Ages* TB/1290

ABBA P. LERNER: Everbody's Business: *A Reexamination of Current Assumptions in Economics and Public Policy* TB/3051

W. ARTHUR LEWIS: Economic Survey, 1919-1939 TB/1446

W. ARTHUR LEWIS: The Principles of Economic Planning. *New Introduction by the Author°* TB/1436

ROBERT GREEN MC CLOSKEY: American Conservatism in the Age of Enterprise TB/1137

PAUL MANTOUX: The Industrial Revolution in the Eighteenth Century: *An Outline of the Beginnings of the Modern Factory System in England°* TB/1079

WILLIAM MILLER, Ed.: Men in Business: *Essays on the Historical Role of the Entrepreneur* TB/1081

GUNNAR MYRDAL: An International Economy. *New Introduction by the Author* TB/1445

HERBERT A. SIMON: The Shape of Automation: *For Men and Management* TB/1245

PERRIN STRYKER: The Character of the Executive: *Eleven Studies in Managerial Qualities* TB/1041

RICHARD S. WECKSTEIN, Ed.: Expansion of World Trade and the Growth of National Economies ** TB/1373

### Education

JACQUES BARZUN: The House of Intellect TB/1051

RICHARD M. JONES, Ed.: Contemporary Educational Psychology: *Selected Readings* ** TB/1292

CLARK KERR: The Uses of the University TB/1264

### Historiography and History of Ideas

HERSCHEL BAKER: The Image of Man: *A Study of the Idea of Human Dignity in Classical Antiquity, the Middle Ages, and the Renaissance* TB/1047

J. BRONOWSKI & BRUCE MAZLISH: The Western Intellectual Tradition: *From Leonardo to Hegel* TB/3001

EDMUND BURKE: On Revolution. Ed. by Robert A. Smith TB/1401

WILHELM DILTHEY: Pattern and Meaning in History: *Thoughts on History· and Society.° Edited with an Intro. by H. P. Rickman* TB/1075

ALEXANDER GRAY: The Socialist Tradition: *Moses to Lenin °* TB/1375

J. H. HEXTER: More's Utopia: *The Biography of an Idea. Epilogue by the Author* TB/1195

H. STUART HUGHES: History as Art and as Science: *Twin Vistas on the Past* TB/1207

ARTHUR O. LOVEJOY: The Great Chain of Being: *A Study of the History of an Idea* TB/1009

JOSE ORTEGA Y GASSET: The Modern Theme. *Introduction by Jose Ferrater Mora* TB/1038

RICHARD H. POPKIN: The History of Scepticism from Erasmus to Descartes. *Revised Edition* TB/1391

G. J. RENIER: History: *Its Purpose and Method* TB/1209

MASSIMO SALVADORI, Ed.: Modern Socialism # HR/1374

GEORG SIMMEL et al.: Essays on Sociology, Philosophy and Aesthetics. *Edited by Kurt H. Wolff* TB/1234

BRUNO SNELL: The Discovery of the Mind: *The Greek Origins of European Thought* TB/1018

W. WARREN WAGER, ed.: European Intellectual History Since Darwin and Marx TB/1297

W. H. WALSH: Philosophy of History: In Introduction TB/1020

### History: General

HANS KOHN: The Age of Nationalism: *The First Era of Global History* TB/1380

BERNARD LEWIS: The Arabs in History TB/1029

BERNARD LEWIS: The Middle East and the West ° TB/1274

### History: Ancient

A. ANDREWS: The Greek Tyrants TB/1103

ERNST LUDWIG EHRLICH: A Concise History of Israel: *From the Earliest Times to the Destruction of the Temple in A.D. 70 °* TB/128

ADOLF ERMAN, Ed.: The Ancient Egyptians: *A Sourcebook of their Writings. New Introduction by William Kelly Simpson* TB/1233

THEODOR H. GASTER: Thespis: *Ritual Myth and Drama in the Ancient Near East* TB/1281

MICHAEL GRANT: Ancient History ° TB/1190

A. H. M. JONES, Ed.: A History of Rome through the Fifgth Century # *Vol. I: The Republic* HR/1364
*Vol. II The Empire:* HR/1460

SAMUEL NOAH KRAMER: Sumerian Mythology TB/1055

NAPHTALI LEWIS & MEYER REINHOLD, Eds.: Roman Civilization *Vol. I: The Republic* TB/1231
*Vol. II: The Empire* TB/1232

### History: Medieval

MARSHALL W. BALDWIN, Ed.: Christianity Through the 13th Century # HR/1468

MARC BLOCH: Land and Work in Medieval Europe. *Translated by J. E. Anderson* TB/1452

HELEN CAM: England Before Elizabeth TB/1026

NORMAN COHN: The Pursuit of the Millennium: *Revolutionary Messianism in Medieval and Reformation Europe* TB/1037

G. G. COULTON: Medieval Village, Manor, and Monastery HR/1022

HEINRICH FICHTENAU: The Carolingian Empire: *The Age of Charlemagne. Translated with an Introduction by Peter Munz* TB/1142

GALBERT OF BRUGES: The Murder of Charles the Good: *A Contemporary Record of Revolutionary Change in 12th Century Flanders. Translated with an Introduction by James Bruce Ross* TB/1311

F. L. GANSHOF: Feudalism TB/1058

F. L. GANSHOF: The Middle Ages: *A History of International Relations. Translated by Rémy Hall* TB/1411

W. O. HASSALL, Ed.: Medieval England: *As Viewed by Contemporaries* TB/1205

DENYS HAY: The Medieval Centuries ° TB/1192

DAVID HERLIHY, Ed.: Medieval Culture and Society # HR/1340

4

J. M. HUSSEY: The Byzantine World  TB/1057
ROBERT LATOUCHE: The Birth of Western Economy: *Economic Aspects of the Dark Ages* °  TB/1290
HENRY CHARLES LEA: The Inquisition of the Middle Ages. || *Introduction by Walter Ullmann*  TB/1456
FERDINAND LOT: The End of the Ancient World and the Beginnings of the Middle Ages. *Introduction by Glanville Downey*  TB/1044
H. R. LOYN: The Norman Conquest  TB/1457
ACHILLE LUCHAIRE: Social France at the time of Philip Augustus. *Intro. by John W. Baldwin*  TB/1314
GUIBERT DE NOGENT: Self and Society in Medieval France: *The Memoirs of Guibert de Nogent.* || *Edited by John F. Benton*  TB/1471
MARSILIUS OF PADUA: The Defender of Peace. *The Defensor Pacis. Translated with an Introduction by Alan Gewirth*  TB/1310
CHARLES PETET-DUTAILLIS: The Feudal Monarchy in France and England: *From the Tenth to the Thirteenth Century* °  TB/1165
STEVEN RUNCIMAN: A History of the Crusades Vol. I: *The First Crusade and the Foundation of the Kingdom of Jerusalem. Illus.*  TB/1143
Vol. II: *The Kingdom of Jerusalem and the Frankish East 1100-1187. Illus.*  TB/1243
Vol. III: *The Kingdom of Acre and the Later Crusades. Illus.*  TB/1298
J. M. WALLACE-HADRILL: The Barbarian West: *The Early Middle Ages, A.D. 400-1000*  TB/1061

*History: Renaissance & Reformation*

JACOB BURCKHARDT: The Civilization of the Renaissance in Italy. *Introduction by Benjamin Nelson and Charles Trinkaus. Illus.* Vol. I TB/40; Vol. II TB/41
JOHN CALVIN & JACOPO SADOLETO: A Reformation Debate. *Edited by John C. Olin*  TB/1239
FEDERICO CHABOD: Machiavelli and the Renaissance  TB/1193
THOMAS CROMWELL: Thomas Cromwell on Church and Commonwealth,: *Selected Letters 1523-1540.* ¶ *Ed. with an Intro. by Arthur J. Slavin*  TB/1462
R. TREVOR DAVIES: The Golden Century of Spain, 1501-1621 °  TB/1194
J. H. ELLIOTT: Europe Divided, 1559-1598 *a* °  TB/1414
G. R. ELTON: Reformation Europe, 1517-1559 ° *a*  TB/1270
DESIDERIUS ERASMUS: Christian Humanism and the Reformation: *Selected Writings. Edited and Translated by John C. Olin*  TB/1166
DESIDERIUS ERASMUS: Erasmus and His Age: *Selected Letters. Edited with an Introduction by Hans J. Hillerbrand. Translated by Marcus A. Haworth*  TB/1461
WALLACE K. FERGUSON et al.: Facets of the Renaissance  TB/1098
WALLACE K. FERGUSON et al.: The Renaissance: *Six Essays. Illus.*  TB/1084
FRANCESCO GUICCIARDINI: History of Florence. *Translated with an Introduction and Notes by Mario Domandi*  TB/1470
WERNER L. GUNDERSHEIMER, Ed.: French Humanism, 1470-1600. * *Illus.*  TB/1473
MARIE BOAS HALL, Ed.: Nature and Nature's Laws: *Documents of the Scientific Revolution* #  HR/1420
HANS J. HILLERBRAND, Ed., The Protestant Reformation #  HR/1342
JOHAN HUIZINGA: Erasmus and the Age of Reformation. *Illus.*  TB/19

JOEL HURSTFIELD: The Elizabethan Nation  TB/1312
JOEL HURSTFIELD, Ed.: The Reformation Crisis  TB/1267
PAUL OSKAR KRISTELLER: Renaissance Thought: *The Classic, Scholastic, and Humanist Strains*  TB/1048
PAUL OSKAR KRISTELLER: Renaissance Thought II: *Papers on Humanism and the Arts*  TB/1163
PAUL O. KRISTELLER & PHILIP P. WIENER, Eds.: Renaissance Essays  TB/1392
DAVID LITTLE: Religion, Order and Law: *A Study in Pre-Revolutionary England.* § *Preface by R. Bellah*  TB/1418
NICCOLO MACHIAVELLI: History of Florence and of the Affairs of Italy: *From the Earliest Times to the Death of Lorenzo the Magnificent. Introduction by Felix Gilbert*  TB/1027
ALFRED VON MARTIN: Sociology of the Renaissance. ° *Introduction by W. K. Ferguson*  TB/1099
GARRETT MATTINGLY et al.: Renaissance Profiles. *Edited by J. H. Plumb*  TB/1162
J. E. NEALE: The Age of Catherine de Medici °  TB/1085
J. H. PARRY: The Establishment of the European Hegemony: 1415-1715: *Trade and Exploration in the Age of the Renaissance*  TB/1045
J. H. PARRY, Ed.: The European Reconnaissance: *Selected Documents* #  HR/1345
BUONACCORSO PITTI & GREGORIO DATI: Two Memoirs of Renaissance Florence: *The Diaries of Buonaccorso Pitti and Gregorio Dati. Edited with Intro. by Gene Brucker. Trans. by Julia Martines*  TB/1333
J. H. PLUMB: The Italian Renaissance: *A Concise Survey of Its History and Culture*  TB/1161
A. F. POLLARD: Henry VIII. *Introduction by A. G. Dickens.* °  TB/1249
RICHARD H. POPKIN: The History of Scepticism from Erasmus to Descartes  TB/139
PAOLO ROSSI: Philosophy, Technology, and the Arts, in the Early Modern Era 1400-1700. || *Edited by Benjamin Nelson. Translated by Salvator Attanasio*  TB/1458
FERDINAND SCHEVILL: The Medici. *Illus.* TB/1010
FERDINAND SCHEVILL: Medieval and Renaissance Florence. *Illus.* Vol. I: *Medieval Florence*  TB/1090
Vol. II: *The Coming of Humanism and the Age of the Medici*  TB/1091
R. H. TAWNEY: The Agrarian Problem in the Sixteenth Century. *Intro. by Lawrence Stone*  TB/1315
H. R. TREVOR-ROPER: The European Witch-craze of the Sixteenth and Seventeenth Centuries and Other Essays °  TB/1416
VESPASIANO: Rennaissance Princes, Popes, and XVth Century: *The Vespasiano Memoirs. Introduction by Myron P. Gilmore. Illus.*  TB/1111

*History: Modern European*

RENE ALBRECHT-CARRIE, Ed.: The Concert of Europe #  HR/1341
MAX BELOFF: The Age of Absolutism, 1660-1815  TB/1062
OTTO VON BISMARCK: Reflections and Reminiscences. *Ed. with Intro. by Theodore S. Hamerow* ¶  TB/1357
EUGENE C. BLACK, Ed.: British Politics in the Nineteenth Century #  HR/1427

5

W. J. BATE: From Classic to Romantic: *Premises of Taste in Eighteenth Century England*
TB/1036

VAN WYCK BROOKS: Van Wyck Brooks: The Early Years: *A Selection from his Works, 1908-1921 Ed. with Intro. by Claire Sprague*
TB/3082

ERNST R. CURTIUS: European Literature and the Latin Middle Ages. *Trans. by Willard Trask*
TB/2015

RICHMOND LATTIMORE, Translator: The Odyssey of Homer
TB/1389

JOHN STUART MILL: On Bentham and Coleridge. *Introduction by F. R. Leavis*
TB/1070

SAMUEL PEPYS: The Diary of Samual Pepys. ° *Edited by O. F. Morshead. 60 illus. by Ernest Shepard*
TB/1007

ROBERT PREYER, Ed.: Victorian Literature **
TB/1302

ALBION W. TOURGEE: A Fool's Errand: *A Novel of the South during Reconstruction. Intro. by George Fredrickson*
TB/3074

BASIL WILEY: Nineteenth Century Studies: *Coleridge to Matthew Arnold* °
TB/1261

RAYMOND WILLIAMS: Culture and Society, 1780-1950 °
TB/1252

## Philosophy

HENRI BERGSON: Time and Free Will: *An Essay on the Immediate Data of Consciousness* °
TB/1021

LUDWIG BINSWANGER: Being-in-the-World: *Selected Papers. Trans. with Intro. by Jacob Needleman*
TB/1365

H. J. BLACKHAM: Six Existentialist Thinkers: *Kierkegaard, Nietzsche, Jaspers, Marcel, Heidegger, Sartre* °
TB/1002

J. M. BOCHENSKI: The Methods of Contemporary Thought. *Trans. by Peter Caws*
TB/1377

CRANE BRINTON: Nietzsche. *Preface, Bibliography, and Epilogue by the Author*
TB/1197

ERNST CASSIRER: Rousseau, Kant and Goethe. *Intro. by Peter Gay*
TB/1092

FREDERICK COPLESTON, S. J.: Medieval Philosophy
TB/376

F. M. CORNFORD: From Religion to Philosophy: *A Study in the Origins of Western Speculation* §
TB/20

WILFRID DESAN: The Tragic Finale: *An Essay on the Philosophy of Jean-Paul Sartre*
TB/1030

MARVIN FARBER: The Aims of Phenomenology: *The Motives, Methods, and Impact of Husserl's Thought*
TB/1291

MARVIN FARBER: Basic Issues of Philosophy: *Experience, Reality, and Human Values*
TB/1344

MARVIN FARBER: Phenomenology and Existence: *Towards a Philosophy within Nature*
TB/1295

PAUL FRIEDLANDER: Plato: *An Introduction*
TB/2017

MICHAEL GELVEN: A Commentary on Heidegger's "Being and Time"
TB/1464

J. GLENN GRAY: Hegel and Greek Thought
TB/1409

W. K. C. GUTHRIE: The Greek Philosophers: *From Thales to Aristotle* °
TB/1008

G. W. F. HEGEL: On Art, Religion Philosophy: *Introductory Lectures to the Realm of Absolute Spirit. ‖ Edited with an Introduction by J. Glenn Gray*
TB/1463

G. W. F. HEGEL: Phenomenology of Mind. ° ‖ *Introduction by George Lichtheim*
TB/1303

MARTIN HEIDEGGER: Discourse on Thinking. *Translated with a Preface by John M. Anderson and E. Hans Freund. Introduction by John M. Anderson*
TB/1459

F. H. HEINEMANN: Existentialism and the Modern Predicament
TB/28

WERER HEISENBERG: Physics and Philosophy: *The Revolution in Modern Science. Intro. by F. S. C. Northrop*
TB/549

EDMUND HUSSERL: Phenomenology and the Crisis of Philosophy. § *Translated with an Introduction by Quentin Lauer*
TB/1170

IMMANUEL KANT: Groundwork of the Metaphysic of Morals. *Translated and Analyzed by H. J. Paton*
TB/1159

IMMANUEL KANT: Lectures on Ethics. § *Introduction by Lewis White Beck*
TB/105

WALTER KAUFMANN, Ed.: Religion From Tolstoy to Camus: *Basic Writings on Religious Truth and Morals*
TB/123

QUENTIN LAUER: Phenomenology: *Its Genesis and Prospect. Preface by Aron Gurwitsch*
TB/1169

MAURICE MANDELBAUM: The Problem of Historical Knowledge: *An Answer to Relativism*
TB/1338

GEORGE A. MORGAN: What Nietzsche Means
TB/1198

H. J. PATON: The Categorical Imperative: *A Study in Kant's Moral Philosophy*
TB/1325

MICHAEL POLANYI: Personal Knowledge: *Towards a Post-Critical Philosophy*
TB/1158

KARL R. POPPER: Conjectures and Refutations: *The Growth of Scientific Knowledge*
TB/1376

WILLARD VAN ORMAN QUINE: Elementary Logic *Revised Edition*
TB/577

WILLARD VAN ORMAN QUINE: From a Logical Point of View: *Logico-Philosophical Essays*
TB/566

JOHN E. SMITH: Themes in American Philosophy: *Purpose, Experience and Community*
TB/1466

MORTON WHITE: Foundations of Historical Knowledge
TB/1440

WILHELM WINDELBAND: A History of Philosophy
Vol. I: *Greek, Roman, Medieval*
TB/38
Vol. II: *Renaissance, Enlightenment, Modern*
TB/39

LUDWIG WITTGENSTEIN: The Blue and Brown Books °
TB/1211

LUDWIG WITTGENSTEIN: Notebooks, 1914-1916
TB/1441

## Political Science & Government

C. E. BLACK: The Dynamics of Modernization: *A Study in Comparative History*
TB/1321

KENNETH E. BOULDING: Conflict and Defense: *A General Theory of Action*
TB/3024

DENIS W. BROGAN: Politics in America. *New Introduction by the Author*
TB/1469

CRANE BRINTON: English Political Thought in the Nineteenth Century
TB/1071

ROBERT CONQUEST: Power and Policy in the USSR: *The Study of Soviet Dynastics* °
TB/1307

ROBERT A. DAHL & CHARLES E. LINDBLOM: Politics, Economics, and Welfare: *Planning and Politico-Economic Systems Resolved into Basic Social Processes*
TB/1277

HANS KOHN: Political Ideologies of the 20th Century
TB/1277

ROY C. MACRIDIS, Ed.: Political Parties: *Contemporary Trends and Ideas* **
TB/1322

ROBERT GREEN MC CLOSKEY: American Conservatism in the Age of Enterprise, 1865-1910
TB/1137

MARSILIUS OF PADUA: The Defender of Peace. *The Defensor Pacis. Translated with an Introduction by Alan Gewirth*
TB/1310

KINGSLEY MARTIN: French Liberal Thought in the Eighteenth Century: *A Study of Political Ideas from Bayle to Condorcet*
TB/1114

BARRINGTON MOORE, JR.:Political Power and Social Theory: *Seven Studies* || TB/1221

BARRINGTON MOORE, JR.: Soviet Politics—The Dilemma of Power: *The Role of Ideas in Social Change* || TB/1222

BARRINGTON MOORE, JR.: Terror and Progress—USSR: *Some Sources of Change and Stability*

JOHN B. MORRALL: Political Thought in Medieval Times TB/1076

KARL R. POPPER: The Open Society and Its Enemies *Vol. I: The Spell of Plato* TB/1101 *Vol. II: The High Tide of Prophecy: Hegel, Marx, and the Aftermath* TB/1102

CONYERS READ, Ed.: The Constitution Reconsidered. *Revised Edition, Preface by Richard B. Morris* TB/1384

JOHN P. ROCHE, Ed.: Origins of American Political Thought: *Selected Readings* TB/1301

JOHN P. ROCHE, Ed.: American Political Thought: *From Jefferson to Progressivism* TB/1332

HENRI DE SAINT-SIMON: Social Organization, The Science of Man, and Other Writings. || *Edited and Translated with an Introduction by Felix Markham* TB/1152

CHARLES SCHOTTLAND, Ed.: The Welfare State ** TB/1323

JOSEPH A. SCHUMPETER: Capitalism, Socialism and Democracy TB/3008

PETER WOLL, Ed.: Public Administration and Policy: *Selected Essays* TB/1284

## Psychology

ALFRED ADLER: The Individual Psychology of Alfred Adler: *A Systematic Presentation in Selections from His Writings. Edited by Heinz L. & Rowena R. Ansbacher* TB/1154

ALFRED ADLER: Problems of Neurosis: *A Book of Case Histories. Introduction by Heinz L. Ansbacher* TB/1145

LUDWIG BINSWANGER: Being-in-the-World: *Selected Papers. || Trans. with Intro. by Jacob Needleman* TB/1365

ARTHUR BURTON & ROBERT E. HARRIS: Clinical Studies of Personality Vol. I TB/3075 Vol. II TB/3076

HADLEY CANTRIL: The Invasion from Mars: *A Study in the Psychology of Panic* || TB/1282

MIRCEA ELIADE: Cosmos and History: *The Myth of the Eternal Return* § TB/2050

MIRCEA ELIADE: Myth and Reality TB/1369

MIRCEA ELIADE: Myths, Dreams and Mysteries: *The Encounter Between Contemporary Faiths and Archaic Realities* § TB/1320

MIRCEA ELIADE: Rites and Symbols of Initiation: *The Mysteries of Birth and Rebirth* § TB/1236

HERBERT FINGARETTE: The Self in Transformation: *Psychoanalysis, Philosophy and the Life of the Spirit* || TB/1177

SIGMUND FREUD: On Creativity and the Unconscious: *Papers on the Psychology of Art, Literature, Love, Religion.* § *Intro. by Benjamin Nelson* TB/45

J. GLENN GRAY: The Warriors: *Reflections on Men in Battle. Introduction by Hannah Arendt* TB/1294

WILLIAM JAMES: Psychology: *The Briefer Course. Edited with an Intro. by Gordon Allport* TB/1034

C. G. JUNG: Psychological Reflections. *Ed. by J. Jacobi* TB/2001

KARL MENNINGER, M.D.: Theory of Psychoanalytic Technique TB/1144

JOHN H. SCHAAR: Escape from Authority: *The Perspectives of Erich Fromm* TB/1155

MUZAFER SHERIF: The Psychology of Social Norms. *Introduction by Gardner Murphy* TB/3072

HELLMUT WILHELM: Change: *Eight Lectures on the I Ching* TB/2019

## Religion: Ancient and Classical, Biblical and Judaic Traditions

W. F. ALBRIGHT: The Biblical Period from Abraham to Ezra TB/102

SALO W. BARON: Modern Nationalism and Religion TB/818

C. K. BARRETT, Ed.: The New Testament Background: *Selected Documents* TB/86

MARTIN BUBER: Eclipse of God: *Studies in the Relation Between Religion and Philosophy* TB/12

MARTIN BUBER: Hasidism and Modern Man. *Edited and Translated by Maurice Friedman* TB/839

MARTIN BUBER: The Knowledge of Man. *Edited with an Introduction by Maurice Friedman. Translated by Maurice Friedman and Ronald Gregor Smith* TB/135

MARTIN BUBER: Moses. *The Revelation and the Covenant* TB/837

MARTIN BUBER: The Origin and Meaning of Hasidism. *Edited and Translated by Maurice Friedman* TB/835

MARTIN BUBER: The Prophetic Faith TB/73

MARTIN BUBER: Two Types of Faith: *Interpenetration of Judaism and Christianity* ° TB/75

MALCOLM L. DIAMOND: Martin Buber: *Jewish Existentialist* TB/840

M. S. ENSLIN: Christian Beginnings TB/5

M. S. ENSLIN: The Literature of the Christian Movement TB/6

ERNST LUDWIG EHRLICH: A Concise History of Israel: *From the Earliest Times to the Destruction of the Temple in A.D. 70* ° TB/128

HENRI FRANKFORT: Ancient Egyptian Religion: *An Interpretation* TB/77

MAURICE S. FRIEDMAN: Martin Buber: *The Life of Dialogue* TB/64

ABRAHAM HESCHEL: The Earth Is the Lord's & The Sabbath. *Two Essays* TB/828

ABRAHAM HESCHEL: God in Search of Man: *A Philosophy of Judaism* TB/807

ABRAHAM HESCHEL: Man Is not Alone: *A Philosophy of Religion* TB/838

ABRAHAM HESCHEL: The Prophets: *An Introduction* TB/1421

T. J. MEEK: Hebrew Origins TB/69

JAMES MUILENBURG: The Way of Israel: *Biblical Faith and Ethics* TB/133

H. J. ROSE: Religion in Greece and Rome TB/55

H. H. ROWLEY: The Growth of the Old Testament TB/107

D. WINTON THOMAS, Ed.: Documents from Old Testament Times TB/85

## Religion: General Christianity

ROLAND H. BAINTON: Christendom: *A Short History of Christianity and Its Impact on Western Civilization. Illus.* Vol. I TB/131; Vol. II TB/132

JOHN T. MCNEILL: Modern Christian Movements. *Revised Edition* TB/1402

ERNST TROELTSCH: The Social Teaching of the Christian Churches. *Intro. by H. Richard Niebuhr* Vol. TB/71; Vol. II TB/72

## Religion: Early Christianity Through Reformation

ANSELM OF CANTERBURY: Truth, Freedom, and Evil: *Three Philosophical Dialogues. Edited and Translated by Jasper Hopkins and Herbert Richardson* TB/317

MARSHALL W. BALDWIN, Ed.: Christianity through the 13th Century # HR/1468

W. D. DAVIES: Paul and Rabbinic Judaism: *Some Rabbinic Elements in Pauline Theology. Revised Edition* ° TB/146

ADOLF DEISSMAN: Paul: *A Study in Social and Religious History* TB/15

JOHANNES ECKHART: Meister Eckhart: *A Modern Translation by R. Blakney* TB/8

EDGAR J. GOODSPEED: A Life of Jesus TB/1

ROBERT M. GRANT: Gnosticism and Early Christianity TB/136

WILLIAM HALLER: The Rise of Puritanism TB/22

GERHART B. LADNER: The Idea of Reform: *Its Impact on the Christian Thought and Action in the Age of the Fathers* TB/149

ARTHUR DARBY NOCK: Early Gentile Christianity and Its Hellenistic Background TB/111

ARTHUR DARBY NOCK: St. Paul ° TR/104

ORIGEN: On First Principles. *Edited by G. W. Butterworth. Introduction by Henri de Lubac* TB/311

GORDON RUPP: Luther's Progress to the Diet of Worms ° TB/120

## Religion: The Protestant Tradition

KARL BARTH: Church Dogmatics: *A Selection. Intro. by H. Gollwitzer. Ed. by G. W. Bromiley* TB/95

KARL BARTH: Dogmatics in Outline TB/56

KARL BARTH: The Word of God and the Word of Man TB/13

HERBERT BRAUN, et al.: God and Christ: *Existence and Province. Volume 5 of Journal for Theology and the Church, edited by Robert W. Funk and Gerhard Ebeling* TB/255

WHITNEY R. CROSS: The Burned-Over District: *The Social and Intellectual History of Enthusiastic Religion in Western New York, 1800-1850* TB/1242

NELS F. S. FERRE: Swedish Contributions to Modern Theology. *New Chapter by William A. Johnson* TB/147

WILLIAM R. HUTCHISON, Ed.: American Protestant Thought: *The Liberal Era* ‡ TB/1385

ERNST KASEMANN, et al.: Distinctive Protestant and Catholic Themes Reconsidered. *Volume 3 of Journal for Theology and the Church, edited by Robert W. Funk and Gerhard Ebeling* TB/253

SOREN KIERKEGAARD: On Authority and Revelation: *The Book on Adler, or a Cycle of Ethico-Religious Essays. Introduction by F. Sontag* TB/139

SOREN KIERKEGAARD: Crisis in the Life of an Actress, and Other Essays on Drama. *Translated with an Introduction by Stephen Crites* TB/145

SOREN KIERKEGAARD: Edifying Discourses. *Edited with an Intro. by Paul Holmer* TB/32

SOREN KIERKEGAARD: The Journals of Kierkegaard. ° *Edited with an Intro. by Alexander Dru* TB/52

SOREN KIERKEGAARD: The Point of View for My Work as an Author: *A Report to History.* § *Preface by Benjamin Nelson* TB/88

SOREN KIERKEGAARD: The Present Age. § *Translated and edited by Alexander Dru. Introduction by Walter Kaufmann* TB/94

SOREN KIERKEGAARD: Purity of Heart. *Trans. by Douglas Steere* TB/4

SOREN KIERKEGAARD: Repetition: *An Essay in Experimental Psychology* § TB/117

SOREN KIERKEGAARD: Works of Love: *Some Christian Reflections in the Form of Discourses* TB/122

WILLIAM G. MCLOUGHLIN, Ed.: The American Evangelicals: 1800-1900: *An Anthology* TB/1382

WOLFHART PANNENBERG, et al.: History and Hermeneutic. *Volume 4 of Journal for Theology and the Church, edited by Robert W. Funk and Gerhard Ebeling* TB/254

JAMES M. ROBINSON, et al.: The Bultmann School of Biblical Interpretation: New Directions? *Volume 1 of Journal for Theology and the Church, edited by Robert W. Funk and Gerhard Ebeling* TB/251

F. SCHLEIERMACHER: The Christian Faith. *Introduction by Richard R. Niebuhr.*
Vol. I TB/108; Vol. II TB/109

F. SCHLEIERMACHER: On Religion: *Speeches to Its Cultured Despisers. Intro. by Rudolf Otto* TB/36

TIMOTHY L. SMITH: Revivalism and Social Reform: *American Protestantism on the Eve of the Civil War* TB/1229

PAUL TILLICH: Dynamics of Faith TB/42

PAUL TILLICH: Morality and Beyond TB/142

EVELYN UNDERHILL: Worship TB/10

## Religion: The Roman & Eastern Christian Traditions

A. ROBERT CAPONIGRI, Ed.: Modern Catholic Thinkers II: *The Church and the Political Order* TB/307

G. P. FEDOTOV: The Russian Religious Mind: *Kievan Christianity, the tenth to the thirteenth Centuries* TB/370

GABRIEL MARCEL: Being and Having: *An Existential Diary. Introduction by James Collins* TB/310

GABRIEL MARCEL: Homo Viator: *Introduction to a Metaphysic of Hope* TB/397

## Religion: Oriental Religions

TOR ANDRAE: Mohammed: *The Man and His Faith* § TB/62

EDWARD CONZE: Buddhism: *Its Essence and Development.* ° *Foreword by Arthur Waley* TB/58

EDWARD CONZE: Buddhist Meditation TB/1442

EDWARD CONZE et al, Editors: Buddhist Texts through the Ages TB/113

ANANDA COOMARASWAMY: Buddha and the Gospel of Buddhism TB/119

H. G. CREEL: Confucius and the Chinese Way TB/63

FRANKLIN EDGERTON, Trans. & Ed.: The Bhagavad Gita TB/115

SWAMI NIKHILANANDA, Trans. & Ed.: The Upanishads TB/114

D. T. SUZUKI: On Indian Mahayana Buddhism. ° *Ed. with Intro. by Edward Conze.* TB/1403

## Religion: Philosophy, Culture, and Society

NICOLAS BERDYAEV: The Destiny of Man TB/61

RUDOLF BULTMANN: History and Eschatology: *The Presence of Eternity* ° TB/91

RUDOLF BULTMANN AND FIVE CRITICS: Kerygma and Myth: *A Theological Debate* TB/80